WELLES-TURNER MEMORIAL LIBRARY
GLASTONBURY, CT 06033

W9-AXF-394

# LET'S GET CREATIVE!
## WRITING FICTION THAT SELLS

by

## William F. Nolan

DISCARDED BY
WELLES-TURNER MEMORIAL LIBRARY
GLASTONBURY, CT

Quill
Driver
Books
Q

Sanger, California

*Copyright © 2007 by William F. Nolan. All Rights Reserved. No part of this book may be reproduced in any form or by any electronic or mechanical means including information storage and retrieval systems without permission in writing from the publisher, except by a reviewer, who may quote brief passages in a review.*

*Published by Quill Driver Books/Word Dancer Press, Inc.*
*1254 Commerce Way*
*Sanger, California 93657*
*559-876-2180 • 1-800-497-4909 • FAX 559-876-2180*
*QuillDriverBooks.com*
*Info@QuillDriverBooks.com*

Quill Driver Books' titles may be purchased in quantity at special discounts for educational, fund-raising, business, or promotional use. Please contact Special Markets, Quill Driver Books/Word Dancer Press, Inc. at the above address or at **1-800-497-4909**.

**Quill Driver Books/Word Dancer Press, Inc. Project Cadre:**
Mary Ann Gardner, Doris Hall, Stephen Blake Mettee, Carlos Olivas

**ISBN**
**1-884956-50-5**

*Printed in the United States of America*

QUILL DRIVER BOOKS and COLOPHON are trademarks of
Quill Driver Books/Word Dancer Press, Inc.

To order another copy of this book, please call
1-800-497-4909

"Just Like Wild Bob" Copyright © 1964 by Connoisseur Publications. Copyright renewed by William F. Nolan.
"The Party" (short story) Copyright © 1967 by HMH Publishing Company. Copyright renewed by William F. Nolan.
"The Party" (teleplay) Copyright © 1984 by William F. Nolan.
"Lonely Train A'Comin'" Copyright © 1984 by William F. Nolan
"The Pool" (as: "A Dip in the Pool") Copyright © 1990 by William F. Nolan
Selections from "Involving Your Reader From the Start" Copyright © 1987 by William F. Nolan.

Library of Congress Cataloging-in-Publication Data

Nolan, William F., 1928-

Let's get creative : writing fiction that sells! / by William F. Nolan.

p. cm.

ISBN 1-884956-50-5

1. Fiction—Authorship. I. Title. II. Title: Let us get creative.

PN3355.N66 2006

808.3—dc22                                    2006020050

*FOR STEVE METTEE*
*FOR CREATIVE REASONS*

## A SPECIAL NOTE OF THANKS

*Let's Get Creative!* has benefited greatly from the many contributions of my wife, writer Cameron Nolan. Aside from keyboarding the entire manuscript on her computer, she added new sections, and substantially improved others through additions and cuts.

Her expert editing is greatly appreciated.

This book would have been much less without Cam's valued input, and she well deserves this special note of thanks.

W.F.N.

# Works by William F. Nolan

The Logan Series
> *Logan's Run* (novel, 1967)
> *Logan's World* (novel, 1977)
> *Logan's Search* (novel, 1980)
> *Logan: A Trilogy* (collection, 1986)
> *Logan's Return* (novella, 2001)
> *The Logan Chronicles* (collection, 2003)
> *Running With Logan* (non-fiction, in progress)

The Black Mask Series
> *The Black Mask Murders* (novel, 1994)
> *The Marble Orchard* (novel, 1996)
> *Sharks Never Sleep* (novel, 1998)

The Sam Space Series
> *Space for Hire* (novel, 1971)
> *Look Out for Space* (novel, 1985)
> *3 For Space* (collection, 1992)
> *Far Out* (collection, 2004)

The Challis Series
> *Death is for Losers* (novel, 1968)
> *The White Cad Cross-Up* (novel, 1969)
> *Helle On Wheels* (novella, 1992)
> *The Brothers Challis* (collection, 1996)

The Kincaid Series
> *Pirate's Moon* (novella, 1987)
> *The Winchester Horror* (novella, 1998)
> *Demon!* (novella, 2006)

On Max Brand
> *Max Brand's Best Western Stories* (Brand collection, 1981)
> *Max Brand's Best Western Stories II* (Brand collection, 1985)
> *Max Brand: Western Giant* (anthology/bibliography, 1986)
> *Max Brand's Best Western Stories III* (Brand collection, 1987)
> *Tales of the Wild West* (Brand collection, 1997)
> *More Tales of the Wild West* (Brand collection, 1999)
> *Masquerade* (Brand collection, 2006)
> *King of the Pulps* (biography, in progress)

On Dashiell Hammett
> *Dashiell Hammett: A Casebook* (critical study, 1969)
> *Hammett: A Life at the Edge* (biography, 1983)
> *A Man Called Dash* (biography, in progress)
> *Dash* (stage play, 2004)

On Ray Bradbury
> *Ray Bradbury Review* (anthology, 1952)
> *The Ray Bradbury Index* (pamphlet, 1953)
> *The Ray Bradbury Companion* (bio/bibliography, 1975)

*The Dandelion Chronicles* (pamphlet, 1984)

*The Bradbury Chronicles* (anthology, 1991)

Science Fiction Anthologies

*The Pseudo-People* (1965)

*Man Against Tomorrow* (1965)

*Il Meglio Della Fantascienza* (1967)

*3 to the Highest Power* (1968)

*A Wilderness of Stars* (1969)

*A Sea of Space* (1970)

*The Future is Now* (1970)

*The Human Equation* (1971)

*Science Fiction Origins* (1980)

Science Fiction Collections

*Alien Horizons* (1974)

*Wonderworlds* (1977)

*Wild Galaxy* (2005)

Bibliographies

*The Work of Charles Beaumont* (1986)

*The Work of William F. Nolan* (1988)

Verse

*The Mounties* (broadside, 1979)

*Dark Encounters* (collection, 1986)

*Have You Seen the Wind?* (collection, with prose, 2003)

*Ill Met By Moonlight* (collection, with prose and artwork, 2005)

Auto Racing Works

*Omnibus of Speed* (anthology, 1958)

*Adventure on Wheels* (John Fitch autobiography, 1959)

*Barney Oldfield* (biography, 1961)

*Phil Hill: Yankee Champion* (biography, 1962)

*Men of Thunder* (collection, 1964)

*When Engines Roar* (anthology, 1964)

*Steve McQueen: Star on Wheels* (biography, 1972)

*Carnival of Speed* (collection, 1973)

Horror Works

*The Fiend in You* (anthology, 1962)

*Things Beyond Midnight* (collection, 1984)

*Urban Horrors* (anthology, 1990)

*How to Write Horror Fiction* (reference, 1990)

*Blood Sky* (chapbook, 1991)

*Helltracks* (novel, 1991)

*Night Shapes* (collection, 1995)

*William F. Nolan's Dark Universe* (career collection, 2001)

*Nightworlds* (collection, 2004)

*Nightshadows* (collection, 2007)

*Death Drive* (screenplay, 2006)

Miscellaneous Works

> *A Cross Section of Art in Science-Fantasy* (chapbook, 1952)
>
> *Image Power* (pamphlet, 1988)
>
> *Rio Renegades* (Western novel, 1989)
>
> *California Sorcery* (mixed anthology, 1999)
>
> *Simply An Ending* (pamphlet, 2002)
>
> *With Marlowe in L.A.* (pamphlet, 2003)

Other Collections

> *Impact 20* (mixed short stories, 1963)
>
> *The Edge of Forever* (collection of Chad Oliver stories, 1971)
>
> *Down the Long Night* (crime collection, 2000)
>
> *Offbeat* (collection of Richard Matheson stories, 2002)
>
> *Ships in the Night* (collection, 2005)

Other Biographies

> *John Huston: King Rebel* (1965)
>
> *Sinners and Supermen* (collection, 1965)
>
> *Hemingway: Last Days of the Lion* (chapbook, 1974)
>
> *McQueen* (1984)
>
> *The Black Mask Boys* (collection/anthology, 1985)

Motion Pictures

> *The Legend of Machine-Gun Kelly* (1975)
>
> *Logan's Run* (1976)
>
> *Burnt Offerings* (1976)

Television Works

> *Brain Wave* (*One Step Beyond*, 1959)
>
> *Vanishing Act* (*Wanted: Dead or Alive*, 1959)
>
> *Black Belt* (*Wanted: Dead or Alive*, 1960)
>
> *The Joy of Living* (*Norman Corwin Presents*, 1971)
>
> *The Norliss Tapes* (NBC Movie of the Week, 1973)
>
> *The Turn of the Screw* (ABC miniseries, 1974)
>
> *Trilogy of Terror* (*Millicent and Therese; Julie*) (ABC Movie of the Week, 1975)
>
> *Sky Heist* (NBC Movie of the Week, 1975)
>
> *The Kansas City Massacre* (ABC Movie of the Week, 1975)
>
> *Logan's Run* (pilot for CBS series, 1977)
>
> *First Loss* (*240-Robert*, 1981)
>
> *The Partnership* (*Darkroom*, 1981)
>
> *Terror at London Bridge* (NBC Movie of the Week, 1985)
>
> *Trilogy of Terror II* (*The Graveyard Rats; He Who Kills*) (USA Movie of the Week, 1996)

# WISE WORDS FROM THE MASTERS:
## WRITING ABOUT WRITING

"A professional writer is an amateur who didn't quit."
— Richard Bach

"In order for a writer to do his or her best, the writer must incorporate originality, a prime ingredient for success."
—Robert Bloch

"When a writer is young he feels that what he is going to say is rather silly or obvious or commonplace, and he tries to hide it under baroque ornament. One's ideas, good or bad, should be plainly expressed. I think a writer always begins by being too convoluted."
—Jorge Luis Borges

"Quantity will make for quality. Michelangelo's, da Vinci's, Tintoretto's billion sketches, the quantitative, prepared them for the qualitative, further down the line, single portraits, and landscapes of incredible control and beauty.

A great surgeon dissects and re-dissects thousands of bodies, tissues, organs, preparing thus by quantity for the time when quality counts with a living person under his knife. An athlete may run ten thousand miles in order to prepare for one hundred yards.

Quantity gives experience. From experience alone can quality come."
—Ray Bradbury

"I take great pleasure out of severely cutting first drafts. It's better to have *too* much material for later shaping than not enough. Always have a rough idea of your first paragraph before you sit down to write, and then you won't be trapped into fearing the blank page."
—Ramsey Campbell

"When seriously explored, the short story seems to me the most difficult and disciplining form of prose."
—Truman Capote

"I think [of fiction] in terms of music, and my short stories are written with the same kind of economy. Each note has to count and it must not be superfluous."
—Joyce Cary

"Any man [or woman] who can write a page of living prose adds something to our life. A writer who hates the actual writing, who gets no joy out of the creation of magic by words, to me is simply not a writer at all. The actual writing is what you live for. The rest [of life] is something you have to get through."
—Raymond Chandler

"Fiction is meant to illuminate, to explode, to refresh. I don't think there's any moral philosophy in fiction beyond excellence."
—John Cheever

"I've known writers who were absolutely destroyed by adverse opinion. You should not allow that to happen and if you do, then it's your fault."
—James Dickey

"It doesn't really matter whether you're first rate, second rate, or third rate, but it's of vital importance that the water finds its own level and that you do the very best you can with the powers that are given you."
—Lawrence Durrell

"There is no mechanical way to get the writing done, no short cut. Teach yourself by your own mistakes; people learn only by error. The quality a writer *must* have is objectivity in judging his work, plus the honesty and courage not to kid himself about it."
—William Faulkner

"I have asked a lot of my emotions—one hundred and twenty stories. The price was high because there was one little drop of something not blood, not tears, not my seed, but me more intimately than these, in every story. It was the extra I had."
—F. Scott Fitzgerald

"No tears in the writer, no tears in the reader. No surprise for the writer, no surprise for the reader."
—Robert Frost

"The [writer's] job is to take pieces of life and arrange them on paper, and the more direct their passage from street to paper the more lifelike they should turn out. To give the impression of things happening here and now, to force upon the reader a feeling of immediacy [the writer] must know how things happen, not just how they are remembered in later years, and must write them down that way."
—Dashiell Hammett

"The most important ingredient in writing fiction is that choice is always available. *Who* will? *What* will?"
—Joseph Heller

"From things that have happened and from all things that you know you make something that is not a representation but a whole new thing and if you make it well enough, you give it immortality. That is why you write."
—Ernest Hemingway

"You have the feeling while you're [writing] that it's something on the plus side. You don't ask yourself if it's pleasurable or distasteful. Making yourself write can be painful, and wonderful when you do. The will has asserted itself, and you feel good again."
—Christopher Isherwood

"I think the quality which makes you want to write and be read is essentially a desire for self-exposure. You must really want to tell the truth about yourself."
—James Jones

"Fiction is about the interaction of people, about their complex relationships. The initial reaction that a story *must* elicit from the reader is empathy, the vicarious experience of the feelings, thoughts, and attitudes of another person."
—Dean Koontz

"From the time I was seventeen, I had no larger desire in life than to be a writer, and I wrote a great deal. Through my Sophomore, Junior, and Senior years at Harvard I must have written thirty or forty short stories, a couple of plays, a short novel, then a long novel. I learned to write by writing."
—Norman Mailer

"I used to think that writing would get easier, the more I did it. I was wrong. It's harder now than ever because I keep pushing myself to write on a deeper, more instinctive level. Human experience. Detail. Deep characterization. The innocence of wonder. Writing from the soul. The essence of struggle. All these are important for *any* writer."
—Robert R. McCammon

"Most writing is done away from the typewriter. It occurs in the quiet, silent moments, while you're walking or playing a game or when you're talking to someone you're not vitally interested in. You're working, your mind is working so when you get to the machine it's a mere matter of transfer."
—Henry Miller

"Writers, like all artists, are concerned to create a more absolute and complete reality than reality itself. I trust in inspiration, which sometimes comes and sometimes doesn't. But I don't sit back waiting for it. I work *every* day."
—Alberto Moravia

"Life is energy, and energy is creativity. And even when we as individuals pass on, the energy is retained in the work, locked in and awaiting release if only someone will take the time and the care to unlock it."
—Joyce Carol Oates

"Anyone who has survived childhood has enough information about life to last for the rest of his [or her] days."
—Flannery O'Connor

"I wrote lyric poetry for a long time, then discovered that God had not intended me to be a lyric poet and the nearest thing to that is the short story [which I now prefer to write]. My own experience with the novel is that it was always too difficult for me to do."
—Frank O'Connor

"The greatness of a writer has nothing to do with subject matter itself, only with how much the subject matter touches the author."
—Boris Pasternak

"Good writing excites me, and makes life worth living. I feel a sense of music continually in writing."
—Harold Pinter

"I look upon literature as an art, and I practice it as an art. Of course, it is also a vocation, and a trade, and a profession, but first it's an art and if you misuse it or abuse it, it will leave you."
—Katherine Anne Porter

"[A writer] must have a continuous curiosity. If he hasn't got that he will wither [plus] a persistent energy. The transit from the reception of stimuli to the recording that is what takes the energy of a lifetime."
—Ezra Pound

"When I'm writing, I know I'm doing the thing I was born to do."
—Anne Sexton

"An absolutely necessary part of a writer's equipment, almost as necessary as talent, is the ability to stand up under punishment, both the punishment the world hands out and the punishment he inflicts upon himself."
—Irwin Shaw

"I think that everyone who does not *need* to be a writer, who thinks he [or she] can do something else, ought to do something else."
—Georges Simenon

"I believe in miracles in every area of life *except* writing. Experience has shown me that there are no miracles in writing. The only thing that produces good writing is hard work."
—Isaac Singer

"It is the duty of the writer to lift up, to extend, to encourage. Great writing has been a staff to lean on, a mother to consult, a wisdom to pick up stumbling folly, a strength in weakness, and a courage to support sick cowardice."
—John Steinbeck

"A great novel should leave you with many experiences, and slightly exhausted at the end. You live several lives while reading it. Its writer should too."
—William Styron

"I write because it's so much fun. When I'm not writing I'm miserable."
—James Thurber

"The author's deepest pride is not in his incidental wisdom but in his ability to keep an organized mass of images moving forward, to feel life engendering itself under his hands."
—John Updike

"You have to write from the inside not the outside, the inside of yourself and of course you have to have common sense enough and structural sense enough to know what is relevant. You don't choose a story, it chooses you."
—Robert Penn Warren

"I like the feeling of being able to confront an experience and resolve it as art, however imperfectly, to give it a form and try to embody it, to hold it and express it in a story."
—Eudora Welty

"Writing brings me not so much pleasure as a deep absorption. My waste-paper basket is filled with work that went a quarter through and which turned out to be among those things that failed to engross the whole of me."
—Thornton Wilder

"All fiction is a kind of magic and trickery a confidence trick, trying to make people believe something is true that isn't."
—Angus Wilson

# CONTENTS

# FOREWORD
## WHY ANOTHER BOOK ON WRITING?

I've been a professional writer for over half a century, and during this period I have examined many books that deal with the craft of fiction. Why another? Why did I write the book you now hold in your hands?

The answer lies in one word: honesty.

I've encountered far too many books that soft-pedal the truth about the creation of professional fiction. They present dishonest information which offers unrealistic hope and false encouragement.

I consider it unethical to encourage a beginner who lacks talent, allowing that person to believe that writing is an easy road to financial success, and that *anyone* can create professional stories and novels. Just because you can write great letters to your grandmother doesn't mean you can write fiction that will sell a process both creative and complex.

I've learned a great deal in my fifty-odd years at the keys, and in these pages I have set out to reveal the truth about the profession of writing. The good and the bad. The bright side and the dark side, too. What you are about to read is, as Hemingway would phrase it, "the true scam."

W.F.N.

# PREFACE
## WHY DO I WRITE, WRITE, WRITE?

Scottsdale, Arizona. I was at a crime-fiction convention and had just finished a reading (two stories and a poem). I was gathering my books and was about to leave the room, when a woman approached me, a questioning look in her eyes.

"Mr. Nolan," she said. "Why do you write, write, write?"

I smiled at her as I replied, "Why do *you* breathe, breathe, breathe?"

That's how vital writing is to me. To me, it is the oxygen of life. I'm not really alive unless I'm writing. I'm compelled to express myself on paper. The words are inside, waiting for me to release them.

Maybe you feel this way, too.

If so, this book should help you breathe.

# Introduction

## Tonight!
### The Secret of Writing

I cannot teach you—or anyone—how to become a professional writer. No one can teach someone else to write. The learning has to come from you—from your strength, talent, and dedication; from your perseverance; and from your willingness to do whatever it takes to reach success.

This book will provide you with the tools for a career in writing. I will tell you what you need to know in order to write professional fiction but it's up to you, and you alone, to get the job done.

When I speak to writing groups, I announce: "Tonight I shall reveal to you the secret of writing." This always elicits intense interest. My audience is eager to know the magic formula.

I say to them: "Here is the secret: You plant your butt in a chair, raise your hands so they hover over the keys, then lower your hands and start clicking away. Do this for at least an hour or two each day for ten years, and you will have learned the secret of writing. The magic formula is: *Work, work, work.*"

They groan. They don't want to hear this. They want to become Stephen King over the weekend.

Well, I tell them, Steve worked for many years to become the writer he is today. He was so poor he lived in a cramped trailer without a telephone. (The service had been cut because of unpaid bills.) To bring in food for his family, he worked in an industrial laundry, writing in his off hours. He was so discouraged after finishing *Carrie* that he tore up the manuscript and tossed it in the wastebasket. His wife found the pages, liked what she read, and pasted them back together.

Doubleday subsequently bought the novel and paperback rights for $400,000. After years of preparation, Stephen King was finally on his way to becoming one of the most popular writers in history.

But he worked hard for it. Night after night. Page after page. Book after book. Year after year.

Yes, he achieved major success. But it *didn't* happen over the weekend.

# I.

# ADVICE TO BEGINNING WRITERS

## IN THE BEGINNING:
### THE ROAD FROM AMATEUR TO PROFESSIONAL

I was born in Kansas City, Missouri, and spent the first nineteen years of my life there. I never dreamed of a professional writing career, yet—from a very early age—I loved to tell stories.

I wrote my first short fiction in a lined Good Value—it cost a nickel!—tablet when I was ten years old. My stories were about cowboys, G-Men, air aces, and superheroes constantly punching and shooting each other. One of my characters from this period, dubbed "The Serpent," was capable of turning himself into a snake to fight crime. (And you may well ask, just how effective a crime-fighting snake is.) I called another of my super-guys "The Flaming Schrab"—because I couldn't spell scarab.

One of the few creative elements about these early efforts was my incredible spelling: "prayie" for prairie, "recestpitll" for respectable, "vanickicked" for vanished, "bnaninds" for bandannas, "sanueted" for sauntered, and "ingasiston" for investigation.

The ending of one of these bullet-ridden epics ("Two Gun Deputy") is typical (with spelling errors intact):

> Just then the girl came up, she said, "Tom—will you stay and be my forman and husband."
>
> Then Tom replied "Im powerful sorry mam, but Im a deputy and I got to be gettin to another town that needs law and oder."
>
> Tom mounted and was off.

When I revisited these juvenile efforts recently, it was tough going for me. They appear to demonstrate *nothing* in the way of future literary promise. Of course, in the way of loving mothers, Mom declared my stories to be "simply wonderful," even if—in truth—they were simply dreadful. But I didn't stop writing. Thank goodness.

I wrote a great deal of inept verse in high school—enough to gain admittance to the National Quill and Scroll Society. (I still don't believe I actually deserved the honor.) And I also began my first novel, a Western I titled *The Trail to Adventure* for which I'm heavily indebted to author Max Brand. The novel was never completed.

And perhaps this is the time for me to talk about beginning writers and novels. If you're a tyro, I have one word for you with regard to starting out your writing career with a novel: *Don't!*

When I was a young man, the fabulously successful writer Ray Bradbury, my close friend for virtually all of my adult life, warned me about attempting to turn out a novel before I was mature enough to understand the mechanics of professional fiction. I was thirty-seven years old before I wrote *Logan's Run*, my first published novel, and by then, I knew exactly what I was doing.

My advice—and Bradbury's—is to start with short stories. A *lot* of short stories.

In 1952, when I first began writing seriously, Bradbury advised me to turn out a new short story every week. "Then, at the end of the year," Ray told me, "you'll have fifty-two bad stories. You'll have purged your system of all the awful stuff. Until you get rid of the bad ones, you won't be able to reach the good ones. And when you make that breakthrough into quality work, you'll know the difference immediately."

Soon after giving me this advice, Ray was on his way to Ireland to adapt *Moby Dick* to the screen for director John Huston. Before he left, Ray told me that when I had a story I felt was of professional quality, I should send it to him. He would read it and tell me if it worked or not.

In the fall of 1953, I did just that, mailing him the final draft of a tale I called "The Joy of Living." It was about a man with young children whose wife had died. At the robot factory he bought a female android to take care of the children while he was on the road. When he came home to stay, he decided it was time to get rid of the robot mother. She pleaded with him to let her stay with the children, saying that she was built to express human emotions and had come to love him and the children. Nevertheless, at the end of my story he took her back to the factory, thinking about her as he drove home, alone, to the children.

Ray congratulated me and praised the story, telling me I'd "done it"—I had reached professional level, but he said the ending was "emotionally wrong." By my story's end, Ray declared, the readers are on the side of the android; they want her to survive. I must *not* have her returned to the factory.

In his letter, Ray laid out the ending he deemed "emotionally correct." I followed it exactly in my revision. I then sent the story to *If: Worlds of SF* and, by golly, they bought it! I still have a copy of that one hundred dollar check on the wall of my office. "The Joy of Living" was printed in the summer of 1954. Thank you, Ray!

Far too many beginning writers become mired in a novel they are unable to finish. Or else they finish it, and, since it's not up to the level of professional, their manuscript is subsequently rejected. Deeply discouraged, they give up on writing as hopeless. This is unnecessary, so long as you realize that novels are for *after* you've taught yourself enough to attempt one with a realistic hope of success.

Luckily, I didn't allow my abortive high school shot at a novel deter me from further prose. But it could have—I was just too ignorant to realize how bad my creative writing was back then.

By my late teens, I focused on becoming a commercial artist. I'd won several prizes for my art. As a result, I was hired as a cartoonist at Hallmark Cards in Kansas City shortly after my high school graduation. I also attended the Kansas City Art Institute. After I moved to California, I established my own art studio in San Diego's Balboa Village, where I painted outdoor murals and sold watercolors. When my one-man show at the Village was praised by the director of the San Diego Fine Arts Gallery, I figured I was on my way.

I was mistaken.

Bottom line: I simply was not talented enough as an artist to earn any kind of decent living. Yet, in January of 1956, in a single hour, I wrote a short story that quickly sold to *Playboy* for five hundred dollars.

Wow! I was stunned. All that money for just an hour's work! Maybe, I thought to myself, writing was what I should be doing instead of art. Maybe I'd been heading in the wrong direction.

Three months later I walked into the office of my boss at the California State Department of Employment, where I was working as a job counselor, and told him that I was quitting to become a full-time writer.

"That's a *terrible* idea," he declared. "You'll starve. Writing is no way to live. Stick to your job here and, in no time at all, you will become a permanent civil servant with a guaranteed income."

"I don't want to become a permanent civil servant," I told him.

He scowled. "Suit yourself, but I can tell you, Nolan, you'll regret this for the rest of your life."

That was nearly fifty years ago, and with eighty books and 1,500 sales behind me, I have yet to regret quitting the California State Department of Employment.

But I wasn't quite as brave as this story makes me sound. I didn't just plunge into the cold sea of professional writing without *some* kind of future income.

It came from my writer-pal Charles Beaumont.

Could be you've never heard of him. For years, he was a fiction "regular" with *Playboy* and he wrote more episodes of *The Twilight Zone* than any other writer except for Rod Serling. Anyway, at that time Beaumont was getting $250 a month for writing a series of lusty personality pieces for *Rogue* magazine under the overall heading "Rogue of Distinction." He had been urging me to quit my office job and write fulltime. When, for the obvious financial reasons, I hesitated, he said: "Look, you can take over my *Rogue* series. This way, you'll be earning at least two-fifty a month."

It was manna from heaven. In the mid-1950s, a beginning writer could live on $250 a month.

Thanks to Ray and Chuck, I was finally on the road from amateur writer to professional.

I never looked back.

## Axioms to Write By

The principles here are basic to writing success. Consider each of them carefully, for they are culled from hard-won experience and knowledge.

1. Unless written for deliberate effect, do not repeat important words in the same sentence.

*Wrong:* He entered the boat and then steered the boat slowly away from shore.

*Right:* He entered the boat and then steered the craft slowly away from shore.

2. Be specific and decisive in your exposition. Don't equivocate. (Although your *characters* may be indecisive and equivocal in both their actions and dialogue.)

3. In most stories, limit your use of profanity and four-letter words. Too many and their shock value is lost. They become boring, redundant, and eventually cast doubt on the writer's ability to be original and creative.

4. Don't show off, or try to be "cute" or precious.

5. Although your characters may use slang as appropriate, be cautious when *you* use it in exposition or when writing as yourself. Be aware that most slang becomes passé fairly quickly. Slang in 1930s *noir* fiction, for example, which was easily understood by all readers of that era, is often confusing or incomprehensible to readers today. If you desire your writing to live beyond your own lifetime, be sparing in your use of slang.

6. Entertain (and subtly instruct) your readers, but never lecture them. Fiction is not the appropriate place for authors to pontificate.

7. Practice writing verse in order to learn compression and economy.

8. Never violate your own moral and ethical code in accepting assignments. I was once asked to write a teleplay called "Death Car on the Freeway"—an easy blueprint for real-life murder, in my opinion. I turned down the offer.

9. If at all possible, write only what excites and intrigues you. If you write against your grain, the result may be professional, but it's very likely to be less than optimally successful.

10. Never discuss an idea or a story with anyone not essential to your project before you've written it. If necessary, you can discuss your ideas and projects-in-progress with collaborators, agents, attorneys, editors, and with as little specific explanation as possible—with those you may need to consult for research purposes. But unless your friends, relatives, romantic interests, work pals, and seatmates on planes or commuter trains fit into one of the above categories, don't say a word about any project you have not yet completed. Talking about a story before it is completed drains off vital creative energy flow, and—as I learned to my detriment—may possibly derail the entire project if you inadvertently talk to someone who is in a position to work against your personal career interests.

# NOVELS AND SHORT STORIES:
## THE DIFFERENCE FOR BEGINNERS

Imagine a large section of dense woods. Then envision a straight path that enters the near edge of these woods and then emerges on the far side.

This straight path is the path of the short story. It leads the reader directly through the woods. No diversions. No side trips. The short story must follow a single track.

The novel takes a far more circuitous route. It enters the woods, then leaves the straight path to explore several side roads. Eventually, it returns to the main path to emerge, at last, on the far side.

Another way to compare the two forms of fiction is to think of a short story as a single, knockout punch in the first round while a novel is a full, fifteen-round bout. In a novel the author has the freedom to move the narrative in several directions, considering each in depth, while the short story demands a much tighter frame in which each incident must lead directly to the climax.

Which is the more difficult form for a writer?

It's a matter of opinion. Some critics point out that the short story requires much greater craft, while a novel is inherently more flexible, allowing the writer far greater latitude in the development of plot and characters.

Both forms are a challenge, and both offer special rewards. Book publishers prefer novels to a collection of short stories by a wide margin, claiming that a novel involves the reader to the fullest extent, while a short story is transitory and fails to satisfy the reader's deeper emotional needs.

Because of this, it is much easier to sell a novel than a collection of short fiction to a publisher, and this often encourages beginning writers to tackle the novel before adequately learning their craft.

But you do not need to write a novel in order to get your work published.

Magazines, fanzines, and other periodicals have traditionally been the first professional venue for beginning writers. Many of these pay the writer in printed copies instead of money, but this doesn't mean they publish bad writing. The editors of these magazines have their personal reputation on the line and the competition to grace their pages is still fierce. This fact is why an author who can list numerous credits in these periodicals can attract the attention of an agent or book publisher. *The International Directory of Little Magazines and Small Presses* is the number-one market guide for these periodicals with more than 6,000 publishers listed. Check the Resources for Writers section at the back of this book for other market guides.

When it comes to book format, I've had over a hundred of my short stories appear in anthologies. Although the editors of anthologies are always looking for "name" writers to headline their books, they also frequently include the work of lesser known—even beginning—writers.

When it comes to collections of work written by one writer, it is rare for a publisher to gamble on a short-story collection until after the author has acquired a reputation and a proven track record of sales.

Yet it's possible to bypass the large, mainline publishers. Once you've established yourself, small presses will often publish collections in limited editions, and these collections frequently include excellent stories that began as early-career magazine sales. I've done this many times, and some of my proudest accomplishments have been small-press editions of my shorter works.*

An additional consideration is the matter of your time. It requires far more time to produce a novel than a short story. Thus, if a novel you have labored over can't find a home with a publisher, it would

---

*Consult *Independent Publisher*, an online magazine listed in the Resources for Writers section in the back of this book, for additional information on small press publication.

likely be far more personally devastating to you than if a short story of yours was rejected.

My advice to you is, don't be lured into attempting a novel until you have perfected your craft by first producing short stories of professional quality. Take the already proven, straight road through those woods until you're confident you won't get lost on a twisting side path.

# THREE 3

## LOGAN'S RUN:
### THE HISTORY OF MY FIRST PUBLISHED NOVEL

Whenever I mention that I wrote *Logan's Run*, I am invariably asked: "How did you sell it? And how did you get it made into a movie and a TV series?"

*Logan's Run* was my first published novel and only my second attempt to write one. It has a history....

The idea behind the novel originated in the summer of 1963, after I'd been writing full-time for seven years. I was in no hurry to tackle a novel, and didn't have one in mind back then.

A friend was teaching a beginner's class in science-fiction writing at UCLA, and he asked me to talk to his students. My assigned topic was to demonstrate the difference between social fiction and science fiction in basic terms the students could understand. I mulled this over and decided to make use of the old cliché *life begins at forty*.

I told the class: "If you write about a man who turns forty, leaves his wife, and runs off with a Vegas showgirl, you're writing social fiction. To create science fiction, reverse this. For instance, you could create an over-populated future society where your protagonist is not allowed to live past forty. If he resists a state-decreed death and runs, he will be hunted down and terminated by a future cop."

I assumed this casually created concept would end there, as a class example, but it stayed with me. I thought, hey, I could get something out of this. I jotted down some notes for a story I intended to call "Killer Man, Killer Man, Leave My Door." With some luck, I thought,

I might sell it for a hundred dollars to *The Magazine of Fantasy and Science Fiction*.

I tested the idea on writer George Clayton Johnson, who had created *Ocean's 11*. George liked it and suggested that we write it together as an original screenplay. I considered this too risky and countered with the suggestion that we do it first as a novel, sell it to a publisher, and *then* write a screen version. He agreed, and we separated to make our individual notes on the idea.

Time passed. We each wrote other things. Then, in the fall of 1965 we got back together, rented a motel room on Pacific Coast Highway in Malibu to use as an office, and sat down to write our novel.

One of the first things we did was to lower the compulsory death age from forty to twenty-one, since it's far more shocking to die just out of your teens, before having had a chance to achieve full maturity. Our two lead characters would be called Logan (after my phone number back in Kansas City: LOgan 6466), and Jessica (after a memorable young woman we knew who had auditioned as a Playboy bunny). I gave my middle name to the Sandman who hunts Logan because I had always strongly disliked being named William *Francis* Nolan.

Logan was a Sandman, a future cop who terminates runners who defy the death-at-twenty-one edict. However, when he turns twenty-one and falls in love with Jessica (the sister of a man he terminated), he too becomes a runner, using his knowledge of the system to stay one jump ahead of his fellow Sandmen. Eventually, Logan and Jess find Sanctuary, where they will be safe; so there is a happy ending. (Far too many science fiction novels, in my opinion, end in doom.)

After we completed the book, we sold it to Dial Press, a publisher with little experience in science fiction. The cover art Dial produced was atrocious. I hate it to this day. Logan and Jess appear as two over-age cancer victims who are running through a city constructed from melting gumdrops.

We began shopping the galleys around to various film agents, asking each of them: "Can you sell this book to a studio for $100,000?" (This was the firm figure we had in mind.) The first two agents said no, but the third said: "Yes, I'm sure I can get you this amount. *Logan's Run* is perfect for films."

The agent sent the galleys to MGM, who agreed it was an ideal screen vehicle. They offered us $65,000 on a Friday. We said no; the price was $100,000. They said they'd get back to us on Monday. We sweated out a long weekend.

Were we crazy? Both George and I needed money, and sixty-five grand back then was big money. Would MGM cancel their offer? Had we killed the goose that was about to lay the golden egg?

But when Monday came, the studio agreed to our full price, and *Logan's Run* became the film property of MGM. It took nine years (and several executive changes) to get the movie produced. At first, George Pal wanted to do it, but after he fell by the wayside, Saul David eventually stepped in as producer. Michael York was cast as Logan and Jenny Agutter as Jessica. Both are classically trained British actors who proved to be superb in their roles.

George and I had written a screenplay that had been purchased as part of a package deal, along with the novel, but in the typical manner of Hollywood, MGM discarded our script and turned the job over to David Z. Goodman, who knew nothing about science fiction. The screenplay he turned out was seriously flawed; it departed radically from the novel in many areas.

People often ask me: "What did you think of the movie?" (It has become a cult classic, with twenty-four Logan web sites around the world). I tell them I liked the first half well enough—that part more or less followed the book—but then...."

The next question is always: "But what did they change?"

"A lot," I reply. "One heck of a lot."

MGM dumbed-down the novel, presenting it solely as action-adventure. The important subtext of the novel, the gradual breakdown of the system due to a lack of maturity, was eliminated by the studio; and the foundational principle that young people alone cannot maintain or develop a successful society was totally ignored in the film.

The compulsory death age was moved from twenty-one up to thirty, which greatly weakened the shock of early death. I was told there were no actors in the novel's age range who could carry a big budget film intended for the general audience. In other words, at that time, no actor that age was an acceptable guarantee to financiers.

George's and my mile-high city became a series of sealed bubble domes—which is silly, since the film demonstrates that the atmosphere outside the domes is fully breathable.

The Sleepshops, where citizens are painlessly euthanized, were turned into the ritual of Carousel, in which thirty-year-olds explode in front of crowds who chant: "Renew! Renew!" The idea was that if a citizen was able to reach the top without exploding, their life would be renewed. But since *everyone* exploded and *no one* was ever renewed, it wasn't logical that the populace would continue to believe in Carousel.

When I pointed out to an MGM executive how illogical this was, he snorted, "Who cares? You don't need logic in science fiction!"

Our deadly, swift-moving character of Box—half-flesh and half-metal—was turned into an awkwardly rolling vanity table with a foil head. Not so deadly, this fellow. In fact, all that was necessary to disable him was to tip him over.

Our Sandman's gun, which fired six potent charges, including a homing bullet that tracked a runner's body heat, became just another zap pistol in the film.

And finally, the novel's entire ending was tossed out and replaced by actor Peter Ustinov, hamming it up as a doddering old man who prattles and natters endlessly about his cats. He totally derailed the movie. "Where in the hell did that old fart come from?" I asked myself.

Ah, well. We got our hundred grand, and that was triumph. And I gained a wonderful "calling card" with Logan. Virtually anyone I've ever talked to has heard of *Logan's Run*. No author could ask for more from one of his literary children.

CBS followed up the film with a watered-down, thirteen-episode TV series for which I wrote the pilot teleplay with Saul David, and the book became a global best-seller, released in twenty-seven editions around the world. As I write this, Warner Bros. is remaking the novel as a major, mega-budget epic, utilizing today's outstanding special effects that were not available in 1975, when MGM originally filmed the book.

After more than forty years, I am proud to say, Logan the Sandman is still running.

# FOUR 4

## IN THE LAND OF YOU:
### CULTIVATING THE INNER SOIL FOR CREATIVE OUTPUT

Every person who reads this book possesses a singular inner landscape: a special land of self, built up incrementally over the years and formed from things done, thoughts entertained, skills learned, places lived, emotions felt, creatures (human and nonhuman) known. Joys, challenges, and sorrows shape this inner landscape. Loves, hates, births, and deaths deepen it. Travel and experience broaden it. Failures and successes expand its horizons. Each hour of life simultaneously forms and modifies it, this land on which we, as writers, must depend for our creative sustenance.

This inner landscape—the land of you—is unique to each writer. From our uniqueness we draw forth the experiences, feelings, descriptions, acts of character, images, opinions, remembered dialogue, and personal philosophy that make up the warp and woof of our creative fabric.

The land of you requires careful tending and constant nourishment.

As each piece of written work is completed and submitted, you transmit to the world a part of yourself, to be weighed and judged, purchased or rejected. Therefore, it's essential that the inner soil you draw from be properly cultivated so it will be capable of supporting an extensive creative output. It is our responsibility as writers to richly seed and care for the land within us.

As a group, writers are usually born imaginative beyond the norm. Throughout our lives, we naturally seek out the dramatic, the bizarre, and the fanciful. When compared to our peers, those who become writers usually read more, dream more, and experience more.

At first, our inner lands are built innocently and unconsciously, because during childhood the inner landscapes under construction are seldom consciously planned. In later years, however, in reflection on their past experiences, writers are usually able to discern the complex, varied, and unique elements which formed each of their singular perspectives.

As a boy growing up in Kansas City, my land was nourished by Alaskan dog stories by James Oliver Curwood and Max Brand's galloping Western novels. Screen idols from Tom Mix to Errol Flynn were part of it, along with comic-book superheroes from Batman to Captain America, old radio shows from *Jack Armstrong, The All-American Boy* to *I Love A Mystery*, as well as countless Saturday afternoon movie theater serials starring Flash Gordon and Tailspin Tommy. Horror films certainly shaped my land. What pop-eyed kid could forget the awesome moment when the unborn monster was raised by a rage of life-giving lightning atop the Frankenstein castle? So, too, did the daily comic strips in the *Kansas City Star*, from "Blondie" to "Terry and the Pirates," help to shape that land. There were World War I two-winger fighting Spads, and pulp magazines, and those fat, fully illustrated Big-Little Books. King Kong was absolutely alive in my imagination; so were Mandrake the Magician, Tom Swift, and Bomba the Jungle Boy. They all contributed to the formation of my inner landscape. Seeing Judy Garland in *The Wizard of Oz* and believing that a witch could fly, listening on the radio to *The Lone Ranger* and being certain that Silver was the greatest horse in the West, reading Tarzan and calmly accepting the fact that a human could be raised by apes—all of these became part of the Land of Me.

And, beyond the things that spurred my imagination, the ordinary events of everyday life contributed their share as well. I remember sledding in the winter, delivering groceries in my red wagon at the age of ten, building my first wooden racer with Dad, skating, swimming, and biking, the years of early schooling, the jobs worked, the friends made. The sad times, and the joyous ones.

As writers, we must preserve the things of our past, while continuing to embrace a constant host of new experiences as our futures unfold, because we will eventually utilize every precious particle of these inner treasures.

Since art is created out of personal perception and experience, our words inscribed on paper must be drawn from this place of self.

A few years ago, because I felt it was time to do so, I drove my car across the face of the nation—from Los Angeles to New York City—in an attempt to absorb new facets of this country. My outer impressions of the physical land I traveled, the new people I met, and what I saw, felt, and experienced became transformed into a permanent part of my inner being.

Arriving at last in New York, I challenged myself: Could I render into words what I had observed on this coast-to-coast journey? Here is some of what I wrote:

Driving the loop of highway through cake-sliced mountains with clumps of distant trees like herds of green sheep grazing the hillsides...a rust-red snake of train, silent in the Arizona heat...snow-patched pine woods into Flagstaff...the timeless, sculptured-granite country of New Mexico...the proud Indian with the scabbed lips on the street in Gallup, walking his straight-backed wife with blind eyes...Government house in Santa Fe, with 300 years of Spanish, Mexican, and American history etched into its adobe pores...the La Fonda Hotel, with its dark, wood-carved interior...on up, into the small New Mexico villages and the old churches with tilting wooden floors and blood-painted Christs...into Taos, and the dirt streets leading to the pueblo beyond town, with its old women huddled on rooftops, wrapped in blankets and silence...through the lush, tight-winding road to Raton and the old dead hotel at Colfax Junction, adrift among piñon and juniper trees...the high, cathedral cliffs orange with sun...on into northern Texas and the crumbling little towns, scoured of paint by wind and rain...and the sadness of Easter morning in Dealey Plaza where JFK's ghost still rides the black death car...into greener, softer country around Austin, and the great, pink-granite Capitol building there...on to San Antonio and the

Alamo, overlaid with Texas commercialism…into Louisiana and the French Quarter of New Orleans, the narrow night streets loud with jazz and tourist laughter…the sudden, stabbing downrush of rain on the highway into Mississippi, erasing reality…the long run along the sun-spangled Gulf of Mexico, with its tall, white-pillared mansions facing the shore like landbound ships, proud with greenery…the sadness of the Southern Gulf cities with their eternal, red-brick structures, dark with time and decay…the blinding Alabama fog outside Montgomery…into Atlanta, graceful with hills, its beauty scarred by acres of poverty…the under-surface hostility of Greenville, North Carolina, and its aimless Southern boys drinking canned beer in their Friday-night cars… along shiny asphalt roads flanked by time-blackened shacks squatting fearfully behind neat white Colonial houses…past wedding-white plum trees into Old Salem and its recreated Yesterday streets…on to the wind-chilled Atlantic Coast and Virginia Beach, past sand-duned woods to the incredible finger of steel and concrete leading into Chesapeake Bay…and down the smooth run through Maryland and Delaware into Washington, a soft, green, beautiful, violent city …to Baltimore, with its endless rows of identical, worn-brick apartment buildings…on to the flat gray terrain of New Jersey…then, cannon-shot, into the clash and impact of New York City via the George Washington Bridge…the snake-tangle of traffic in the canyoned streets…and the final—almost unreal—quiet of a late-night, Manhattan hotel room.

These were the words I typed as I sat in that New York hotel. They are a sample of *self*: personal, prejudiced, immediate, drawn from the Land of Me.

No two lands can ever be alike, since no two writers are alike. My land is a productive one because I insure that its soil, renewed regularly, is always rich and able to produce the harvest of words I require of it each year.

In order to generate this richness from which we draw our fiction, we must become aware of the infinite possibilities around us.

Listen—really *listen*—to that talkative waitress the next time you sit at a restaurant counter.

Find out *why* you're so happy sailing on a clear lake at sundown...or *why* the wind has a special, sweet taste in spring...or *why* the laughter of your child pleases you.

Analyze the everyday, often trivial, moments of your life—from your regular trip out to empty the trash to the routine, twice-daily ride in your office elevator.

Discover what elements of life move you, irritate you, delight you. Take nothing for granted. Constantly examine the texture of your life, and the life that occurs around you.

Pay attention to *all* of your senses—sight, hearing, smell, taste, and touch. In ordinary circumstances, most of us are habitually aware of just one or two. Become alert to every sense you are able to access, including your psychic senses, if you are aware of them.

Keep all of your creative pores open to insure a rich and constantly renewed inner landscape.

That unique creative landscape which is The Land of You.

# A BASIC REQUIREMENT:
## READ! READ! READ!

Once when I was attending a fantasy convention in Rhode Island, a woman approached me and said she wanted to become a horror writer.

"Great," I said. "Do you read horror fiction?"

"Oh, yes," she declared. "I've read everything by Stephen King."

"And what other writers do you read?" I inquired.

"None," she told me. "Just Stephen King."

I was stunned. Writing classes, book conventions, and self-help books can never replace the value of constant reading. To become a writer—*any* kind of writer—requires constant reading across an extremely wide spectrum of literature. Everyone who reads this book should be familiar with literally hundreds of authors from past and present, from Shakespeare to Defoe, Austen to Poe, Hemingway to Robert Heinlein, Amy Tan to J. K. Rowling. From period to contemporary, from classics to pop culture. The best way to learn to write is: Read! Read! Read!

Learn from the masters. Discover how professional writers handle plot, dialogue, characterization, conflict, and description. Dissect their short stories and novels. Use what you read as fuel for your imagination. *Feed* on good writing, which is the nourishment required for your creative soul.

I began reading Batman comics when I was very young. I graduated to Big-Little Books, Tom Swift, and Bomba the Jungle Boy, then went on to H. G. Wells and Jack London, and—eventually—to modern masters such as Hemingway, F. Scott Fitzgerald, Truman Capote, and Faulkner.

My personal reading includes horror, fantasy, science fiction, mysteries, and mainstream fiction—with a smattering of classics along the way.

A warning: Don't feel that you *must* read the classics in order to write, yet understand that they are called classics because they have enduring literary value. A sampling will tell you which classic authors resonate with you and which do not. Some are indeed heavy going: I gave up on *Moby Dick* at the halfway mark. The book, as the old story goes, told me more about whales than I cared to know.

And, hey! If you don't like reading Shakespeare (personally, I prefer watching his plays), don't feel compelled to read him. You can always come back to Shakespeare—or any other classic author—at a future time. He will still be around.

I learned about humor from Perelman and Thurber, about hard-knuckled action from Hammett and Chandler, about poetic prose from Bradbury and Capote, about wartime courage from Mailer and Hemingway, about the future from Heinlein and Clarke, and about human adversity from Fitzgerald and Steinbeck. There is a huge body of literature available to you, and you must be willing to explore (at least to the extent of dipping in) every part of it.

Read omnivorously, and then gradually focus on what excites you, what turns you on and makes you feel more alive.

I have been asked which book influenced me most as a writer, and I always name *The Sound and the Fury* by William Faulkner. Why? Because in this novel Faulkner taught me that a writer can go much farther out on the literary limb than I had ever before imagined. The first third of the book is told by an idiot, and makes no sense until you've read the last two-thirds of the novel. Faulkner was not afraid to confuse his readers. He trusted them to finish his book and to under-stand his radical approach.

At this point I'm going to list eighty books that changed my life—alphabetically, by author. I'm not suggesting that you read all of them, but sample the ones you're able to find. You won't be sorry, because each of these has special value to writers.

Robert Aickman *The Wine-Dark Sea*
J. G. Ballard *The Crystal World*
Charles Beaumont *The Hunger*
Alfred Bester *The Stars My Destination*
Ray Bradbury *The Martian Chronicles*
Max Brand *The Rancher's Revenge*
Fredric Brown *What Mad Universe*
John Brunner *Stand on Zanzibar*
Anthony Burgess *A Clockwork Orange*
Paul Cain *Fast One*
Truman Capote *A Tree of Night*
Robert W. Chambers *The King in Yellow*
Raymond Chandler *The Big Sleep*
John Cheever *The Stories of John Cheever*
Arthur C. Clarke *Rendezvous With Rama*
Hal Clement *Needle*
John Collier *Fancies and Goodnights*
Joseph Conrad *Heart of Darkness*
James Gould Cozzens *Castaway*
James Oliver Curwood *Kazan*
Philip K. Dick *Do Androids Dream of Electric Sheep?*
Charles Dickens *Oliver Twist*
Arthur Conan Doyle *The Lost World*
Fyodor Dostoyevsky *Crime and Punishment*
Charles Finney *The Circus of Dr. Lao*
F. Scott Fitzgerald *Tender Is the Night*
Ian Fleming *From Russia With Love*
William Golding *Lord of the Flies*
William Goldman *Marathon Man*
Nadine Gordimer *The Soft Voice of the Serpent*
Joe Gores *A Time of Predators*
Davis Grubb *Night of the Hunter*
Dashiell Hammett *The Maltese Falcon*
Thomas Harris *The Silence of the Lambs*
Robert A. Heinlein *The Green Hills of Earth*
Joseph Heller *Catch 22*
Ernest Hemingway *For Whom the Bell Tolls*

William Hjortsberg *Falling Angel*
Aldous Huxley *Brave New World*
Shirley Jackson *The Bird's Nest*
Henry James *The Turn of the Screw*
Franz Kafka *The Castle*
Stephen King *The Shining*
Nigel Kneale *Tomato Cain*
Dean Koontz *Intensity*
Joe Lansdale *The Nightrunners*
Fritz Leiber *Conjure Wife*
Ira Levin *A Kiss Before Dying*
Jack London *White Fang*
Norman Mailer *The Armies of the Night*
W. Somerset Maugham *Cakes and Ale*
Richard Matheson *Bid Time Return*
A. Merritt *The Ship of Ishtar*
Arthur Miller *Death of a Salesman*
Ward Moore *Greener Than You Think*
Vladimir Nabakov *Lolita*
Joyce Carol Oates *Black Water*
John O'Hara *Appointment in Samarra*
George Orwell *Nineteen Eighty-Four*
S.J. Perelman *Crazy Like a Fox*
J. D. Salinger *The Catcher in the Rye*
Budd Schulberg *The Disenchanted*
Irwin Shaw *Mixed Company*
Robert Sheckley *Mindswap*
Clifford D. Simak *City*
John Steinbeck *East of Eden*
George R. Stewart *The Earth Abides*
Bram Stoker *Dracula*
Peter Straub *Floating Dragon*
Theodore Sturgeon *More Than Human*
James Thurber *My Life and Hard Times*
Wilson Tucker *The Long, Loud Silence*
H. G. Wells *The War of the Worlds*
Eudora Welty *A Curtain of Green*

Nathanael West *The Day of the Locust*
Jack Williamson *The Humanoids*
F. Paul Wilson *The Touch*
Cornell Woolrich *Night Has a Thousand Eyes*
Philip Wylie *The Disappearance*
Roger Zelazny *Damnation Alley*

# SIX 6

## FINDING THE TIME TO WRITE:
### ELIMINATE THE TIME WASTERS

"You know, Mr. Nolan, I'd love to write—and I've thought a lot about it—but I have a job and a family and there's just no time left over."

When I ask for a brief description of a typical day, almost invariably the Internet takes up a minimum of an hour or two a day—and sometimes several more unnoticed hours. But people often think that online time—especially while at work or after dark— somehow doesn't "count." There's television, often explained to me as: "But I *must* look at the news and the talking-heads programs to know what's going on."

There's totally unnecessary energy spent with instant messaging and cell phones: "Hi. Howzit going? I'm on my way to the store now. Just passing Greenwood Avenue. Hey! Guy back there just ran the light. Jeez, what an idiot! Thought I'd pick up some pasta at the deli for dinner, been thinking about manicotti all day. Sound okay? Yeah? What about salad dressing?" Not to mention all the time spent listening to the trivia, depressing and irritating ads, destructive "humor," dreary d.j.'s, offensive talkmeisters, repetitive shortlist music selections, and idiotic call-in listeners during drive-time radio hours.

"You have no time for writing?" I ask.

"That's right. Just no time at all for it."

"That's bull," I say.

Shock. The would-be writer stares at me.

"Ration your time on the Internet. Check your email two, three times max. Stay out of time-wasting chatrooms and stupid forums.

They're addictive, and they fritter away your existence while giving the illusion that you're living a life. Instead of watching television, use Yahoo to check the day's headlines and you'll stay right up to date on anything you need to know. Cancel your TV cable service (which will save you a chunk of money), and unplug your TV set. Avoid cell-phone calls and instant messaging unless it's an emergency. Tune your radio to the classical station, or turn it off. If you need to, carry a pocket recorder with you so you can speak your 'writing' as you drive. You'll go through withdrawal pains, just like anyone who's addicted, but in a short period of time, you'll discover that you've easily freed up two or more hours a day that you can use to write or to think about writing. Realize that even if you only produce a single page a day of new writing, that's 365 pages—over 80,000 words—at the end of each year. And that's significant."

More than a half-century ago, during the 1950s, Elmore Leonard, author of *Hombre*, *Get Shorty*, and dozens of other best-sellers, worked full-time at an ad agency in Detroit. Because his weekends were devoted to his growing family, he thought there was no time for his freelance writing.

"I realized I was going to have to get up at five in the morning if I wanted to write fiction," said Leonard. "It wasn't easy. The alarm would go off and I'd groan, get up, stagger into the living room, and sit down at the table with a yellow legal pad and try to write two pages. Rule was: I had to get those two pages done before I could have my morning coffee. It worked, and I did it that way for most of the fifties."

We all have the same twenty-four hours, but we also currently have more time-wasting distractions—the kind that advertisers and media moguls convince us are "essential" parts of our lives—than ever before in human history. For most people, finding the time you need to write can actually be easy: Just cut out the time-wasters—anything that doesn't generate a warm sense of inner satisfaction that lasts—and use the time you've freed up for writing.

I did. Thousands of others have. And so can you.

# SEVEN 7

## EXPRESSING YOUR INDIVIDUALITY:
### DISCOVER YOUR WORLD

You are unique. You are not your mother or father, sister or brother, wife or husband. A separate universe is contained within your skin. The same is true of every person on this planet. Your task is to discover what is unique about you, and then get it down on paper.

When I began to write, I imitated my early role models: Max Brand, Ray Bradbury, and, to some degree, Ernest Hemingway. In the beginning, when I was untested and unsure of myself, I worked in the shadow of the writers I most admired.

This is common with novice writers. We begin by functioning as followers. Slowly, however, as we gain experience, we begin to express our individuality and we learn to utilize that which is unique in each of us.

It often takes much effort to uncover this special vein of individuality; we must work steadily to clear away the weeds and brush to reach the fertile soil of our own imagination. Since each of us experiences life from a different perspective, no two people will react exactly alike to the same experience.

As writers, we transform our own personal uniqueness into fiction—disguised, quite often, but based on the truths of our inner selves.

There is a King world, and a Bradbury world, and a Hemingway world, but these worlds are not yours. You must discover *your* world and use it to become a writer like no other.

You are one of a kind.

Know it.

Express it.

# EIGHT 8

## DEVELOPING A WRITING STYLE:
### BEING TRUE TO YOURSELF

Style is a concern of many novice writers. "How did you develop *your* style?" they ask me.

My answer is: "I didn't. I let it evolve."

They are confused. How can a writer's style just "evolve"?

The answer is individuality.

Style is a writer's individual expression; it matures naturally out of the writer's personality. Genuine style can't be forced or artificially created.

Hemingway's style developed from his desire to trim the English language of excess verbiage. He developed a bone-sharp method of writing that became his "style."

Ray Bradbury's style developed from his passion for poetic prose.

Raymond Chandler's style is a direct expression of his dark view of crime, mixed with his abiding affection for the wisecrack.

But none of them ever sat down and declared: "Now I am going to create my own special style of writing."

I tell novice writers not to worry about style; it will develop as they write.

Just keep writing and allow the natural process to unfold.

# NINE 9

## DON'T COMPROMISE:
### ONLY CREATIVE INTEGRITY CAN BRING SUCCESS

As a writer, you must maintain your basic integrity: You must be true to what you believe in, and you must write mainly for yourself. If what you write pleases your editors and readers, that's fine. That's the goal. But first you must please yourself.

"Hey!" you tell yourself. "There's a big market out there for junky romance novels, so I'll write one. My stuff can't be any worse than what's already getting published!"

No good. If you compromise your talent, if you deliberately write something you consider "junk," two things will happen: 1) You will have contempt for yourself and suffer a subsequent loss of self-respect for your talent; and 2) You won't sell your "junk."

Why won't you be able to sell your junky romance novel? Because if you talk to successful writers of published romance novels you will learn that they *believe* in what they're doing. They have genuine affection and respect for the genre they are a part of. Check out *Romantic Times* magazine (www.romantictimes.com) and see for yourself.

You, too, must have pride in what you write. If you feel contempt for your work, your effort at *writing-down* to the market will be transparent, and you won't be able to sell. If you attempt to write what is false to you, you'll never achieve writing success.

"But I need to make money from my work," you argue. "I need to reach the commercial markets to survive."

There is nothing wrong with reaching out to the commercial

markets, so long as you maintain your creative integrity. I've written for many commercial markets, but I've given each the best that is in me. I have never deliberately lowered my personal writing or ethical standards.

In the early years of his career, Ray Bradbury tried to distort his natural talent to fit the pulp crime markets, but he was writing against his grain and he had difficulty selling these early stories. "Most of them were forced and artificial," he recalls. He sold a few, but it was only when he began reaching back into his growing-up years, writing about the things that resonated emotionally within him, that he became an original talent who had found his own, special voice. Ray's work took on meaning and depth only when he abandoned his efforts to meet the needs of a market he wasn't suited for.

Have faith in yourself.

Find your own voice.

Don't compromise.

## CLARITY IN PROSE:
### BEING SIMPLE AND DIRECT

*Write clearly!* These are two vital words that should be branded into the mind of every beginning writer. Tell your story directly, with clarity and precision. Avoid being deliberately obscure, tricky, or dense. For beginners who want to become professional writers, clarity is essential.

Yes, Faulkner could be dense, but he was a rare genius and an exception to the rule. You are not William Faulkner. Your words must intrigue and entertain and satisfy your readers. Your sentences must be clear and precise. You dare not leave your readers—particularly those readers who are editors—confused or irritated because they are unable to understand you.

Ernest Hemingway is one of the best examples of writers who spend many years in pursuit of clear, unadorned prose. "I know all the ten-dollar words," he once declared, "but I prefer to use simpler, shorter words."

If a writer does not communicate simply and directly with his readers, he has failed in his role as a storyteller.

When I was on the staff of the Sandhills Writers Conference in Georgia, part of my job was to evaluate the manuscripts of student writers. One manuscript stood out among the lot. The author had created a story that was totally obscured by the use of Hemingway's "ten-dollar words." This young man was desperately anxious to prove he was an intellectual, but the result was an unreadable manuscript.

Don't try to impress the reader with how smart you are, or how many big words you know or can use. Readers buy your work to be entertained (and perhaps enlightened en route), but they will not tolerate overblown, self-conscious writing.

Be simple.

Be direct.

Always strive for clarity.

# ELEVEN 11

## BREAKING THE BLOCK:
### WRITE ANYWAY

Okay, you've been writing every day, but one day you sit down at your keyboard and no words come. Your mind is devoid of ideas. You feel mentally frozen, unable to generate new thoughts or sentences.

You have writer's block.

It happens to all of us at one time or another. For many years, I thought I was immune—that writer's block would never happen to me. But it did. When I moved to Oregon, after more than a half-century in Southern California, I found it extremely difficult to adjust to the sudden dislocation. After I set up my office in the apartment I rented, I found myself unable to write. I felt alien and disconnected—not only from my immediate geographical surroundings, but from my own creative process.

For two months I suffered a classic case of writer's block. Then I got tough with myself.

"Shape up, Nolan!

"You're *not* going to allow a simple change of environment to stop you.

"Write!*Write*, damn you!"

I sat down and started writing. Just made myself write words on paper. And I broke the block.

If you happen to discover, for whatever reason, that you're blocked, force yourself to sit at the keys for at least an hour every day. Type whatever comes into your head. Don't worry about stories or plots, just fire away at the keys. Even if you produce gibberish, that's fine; you're still getting words out. Do this each day and you will soon break the block, ready and able to produce new creative work.

And although this book is about writing fiction, you may find that a bout of writer's block might be the right time for you to turn out some non-fiction work: articles, reviews, or biography. Not only will non-fiction writing keep your creative juices pumping, it can also easily lead to new sources of supplemental income (something all writers appreciate).

Keep in mind that writing is like any other job. If you were being paid to create ad copy, or you were a magazine editor who just <u>had</u> to produce a short story about the upcoming Baja California road rally (because it would subtly tie-in with an important advertising layout in the same issue), you'd figure out a way to do it, whether you were suffering from writer's block or not.

Benefit from what I learned personally: Writer's block can be painful, but if you do the necessary work to break the creative impasse, you will see it is only temporary.

# II.

# A WRITER'S MATERIAL AND TOOLS

# TWELVE 12

## HARVESTING YOUR DREAMS:
### DON'T LET THEM GET AWAY

Several of my best stories have had their origins in dreams. In fact, *Helltracks*, my first horror novel, began as a dream:

A nameless cowboy was waiting on the porch of an abandoned, boarded-up depot on the wide plains of Montana. In the far background, a distant range of mountains ringed the plain. The cowboy's sister had died after boarding a mystery train. He was waiting at the depot so he could kill the train.

Then I woke up. I grabbed the notepad on my bedside table and jotted down everything I could recall from the dream. (Always keep a notepad and pen next to your bed; dreams slip away rapidly.)

When I finished writing, I was awake and intrigued. I asked myself how this cowboy's sister died, who he was, and…how do you "kill" a train?

The answers formed themselves in my mind. I decided to create a *living* train. Problem: How could I convince readers that a train made of metal could achieve organic life? Well…I'd once visited the Petrified Forest in Arizona, where I observed once-living wood that had, over the eons, become transformed into stone. So what if I *reversed* this? What if I had nonliving train metal turn into living tissue?

I worked out my story along these lines: An old steam train from the 1800s, abandoned after the historic Montana mining boom of that era, has been forgotten for more than a century on a remote and forgotten spur track in the mountains. This is an area, I postulated, where the local American Indians believed strange life forms to exist. Since the now-living train requires flesh to feed its dark hunger, it rolls down onto the plains at night to devour the victims who innocently board it, one of whom is my cowboy's sister. The cowboy (a present-day sheep rancher) determines to avenge her death by destroying the train.

After getting this idea, I felt the need to find a realistic locale for the action. I'd never been to Montana, so I drove there from Southern California, searching for an area in which to set my story.

What I discovered totally astonished me: an expanse of flat Montana plain (in sheep ranching territory!), crossed with rail tracks, and ringed by the distant Little Belt Mountains. Most amazing of all, at a place called Ross Fork, I found a boarded-up rail depot, right in the center of the plain.

*Everything* matched my dream, as if I had lived there in an earlier life. (And perhaps I had.)

I wrote my story, called it "Lonely Train A'Comin'" and later developed it into the novel *Helltracks*.

Here's the original…

## Lonely Train A'Comin'

Lonely train a'comin'
I can hear its cry
Lonely train from nowhere
Takin' me to die
—folk ballad fragment, circa 1881

At Bitterroot, Ventry waited.

Bone-cold, huddled on the narrow wooden bench against the paint-blistered wall of the depot, the collar of his fleece-lined coat turned up against the chill Montana winds blowing in from the Plains, he waited for the train. Beneath the wide brim of a work-blackened Stetson, sweat-stained along the headband, his eyes were intense, the gun-metal color of blued steel. Hard lines etched into the mahogany of his face spoke of deep-snow winters and glare-sun summers; his hands, inside heavy leather work gloves, were calloused and blunt-fingered from punishing decades of ranch work.

Autumn was dying, and the sky over Bitterroot was gray with the promise of winter. This would be the train's last run before snow closed down the route. Ventry had calculated it with consummate patience and precision. He prided himself on his stubborn practicality, and he had earned a reputation among his fellow ranchers as a hard-headed realist.

Paul Ventry was never an emotional man. Even at his wife's death he had remained stolid, rock-like in his grief. If it was Sarah's time to die, then so be it. He had loved her, but she was gone and he was alone and that was fact. Ventry accepted. Sarah had wanted children, but things hadn't worked out that way. So they had each other, and the ranch, and the open Montana sky—and that had been enough.

Amy's death was not the same. Losing his sister had been wrong. He did *not* accept it. Which was why he was doing this, why he was here. In his view, he had no other choice.

He had been unable to pinpoint the train's exact arrival, but he was certain it would pass Bitterroot within a seven-day period. Thus, he had brought along enough food and water to last a week. His supplies were almost depleted now, but they could be stretched through two more days and nights if need be; Ventry was not worried.

The train *would* be here.

It was lonely at Bitterroot. The stationmaster's office was boarded over, and bars covered the windows. The route into Ross Fork had been dropped from the rail schedule six months ago, and main-line trains bound for Lewiston no longer made the stop. Now the only trains that rattled past were desolate freights, dragging their endless rusted flatcars.

Ventry shifted the holstered axe pressing against his thigh, and unzipping a side pocket on his coat, he took out the thumb-worn postcard. On the picture side, superimposed over a multicolored panoramic shot of a Plains sunset, was the standard Montana salutation: GREETINGS FROM BIG SKY COUNTRY! And on the reverse, Amy's last words. How many times had he read her hastily scrawled message, mailed from this depot almost a year ago to the day?

*Dear Paulie, I'll write a long letter, I promise, when I get to Lewiston, but the train came early so I just have time, dear brother, to send you my love. And don't worry about your little kid sister because life for me is going to be super with my new job! Luv and XXXXXXX, Amy*

And she had added a quick P.S. at the bottom of the card:

*You should see this beautiful old train! Didn't know they still ran steam locomotives like this one! Gotta rush— 'cuz it's waiting for me!*

Ventry's mouth tightened, and he slipped the card back into his coat, thinking about Amy's smiling eyes, about how much a part of his life she'd been. Hell, she was a better sheep rancher than half the valley men on Big Moccasin! But, once grown, she'd wanted city life, a city job, a chance to meet city men.

"Just you watch me, Paulie," she had told him, her face shining with excitement. "This lil' ole job in Lewistown is only the beginning. The firm has a branch in Helena, and I'm sure I can get transferred there within a year. You're gonna be real proud of your sis. I'll *make* you proud!"

She'd never had the chance. She'd never reached Lewiston. Amy had stepped aboard the train...and vanished.

Yet people didn't vanish. It was a word Paul refused to accept. He had driven each bleak mile of the rail line from Bitterroot to Lewiston, combing every inch of terrain for a sign, a clue, a scrap of clothing. He'd spent two months along that route. And had found nothing.

Ventry posted a public reward for information leading

to Amy's whereabouts. Which is when Tom Hallendorf contacted him.

Hallendorf was a game warden stationed at King's Hill Pass in the Lewis and Clark National Forest. He phoned Ventry, telling him about what he'd found near an abandoned spur track in the Little Belt range.

Bones. *Human* bones.

And a ripped, badly stained leather purse.

The empty purse had belonged to Amy. Forensic evidence established the bones as part of her skeleton.

What had happened up there in those mountains?

The district sheriff, John Longbow, blamed it on a "weirdo." A roving tramp.

"Dirt-plain obvious, Mr. Ventry," the sheriff had said to him. "He killed her for what she had in the purse. You admit she was carryin' several hundred in cash. Which is, begging your pardon, a damn fool thing to do!"

But that didn't explain the picked bones.

"Lotta wild animals in the mountains," the lawman had declared. "After this weirdo done 'er in he just left her layin' there—and, well, probably a bear came onto 'er. It's happened before. We've found bones up in that area more than once. Lot of strange things in the Little Belt." And the sheriff had grinned. "As a boy, with the tribe, I heard me stories that'd curl your hair. It's wild country."

The railroad authorities were adamant about the mystery train. "No steamers in these parts," they told him. "Nobody runs 'em anymore."

But Ventry was gut-certain that such a train existed, and that Amy had died on it. Someone had cold-bloodedly murdered his sister and dumped her body in the mountains.

He closed down the ranch, sold his stock, and devoted himself to finding out who that someone was.

He spent an entire month at the main library in Lewiston, poring through old newspaper files, copying names, dates, case details.

A pattern emerged. Ventry found that a sizable number of missing persons who had vanished in this area of the state over the past decade had been traveling by *rail*. And several of them had disappeared along the same basic route Amy had chosen.

Ventry confronted John Longbow with his research.

"An' just who is this killer?" the sheriff asked.

"Whoever owns the steamer. Some freak rail buff. Rich enough to run his own private train, and crazy enough to kill the passengers who get on board."

"Look, Mr. Ventry, how come nobody's *seen* this fancy steam train of yours?"

"Because the rail disappearances have happened at night, at remote stations off the main lines. He never runs the train by daylight. Probably keeps it up in the mountains. Maybe in one of the old mine shafts. Uses off-line spur tracks. Comes rolling into a small depot like Bitterroot *between* the regular passenger trains and picks up whoever's on the platform."

The sheriff had grunted at this, his eyes tight on Paul Ventry's face.

"And there's a definite *cycle* to these disappearances," Ventry continued. "According to what I've put together, the train makes its night runs at specific intervals. About a month apart, spring through fall. Then it's hidden away in the Little Belt each winter when the old spur tracks are snowed over. I've done a lot of calculation on this, and I'm certain that the train makes its final run during the first week of November—which means you've still got time to stop it."

The sheriff had studied Paul Ventry for a long, silent moment. Then he had sighed deeply. "That's an interesting theory, Mr. Ventry, real interesting. But…it's also about as wild and unproven as any I've heard—and I've heard me a few. Now, it's absolute natural that you're upset at your sister's death, but you've let things get way out of whack. I figger you'd best go on back to your ranch and try an' forget about poor little Amy. Put her out of your mind. She's gone. And there's nothing you can do about that."

"We'll see," Ventry had said, a cutting edge to his voice. "We'll see what I can do."

Ventry's plan was simple. Stop the train, board it, and kill the twisted son of a bitch who owned it. Put a .45 slug in his head. Blow his fucking brains out—and blow his train up with him!

I'll put an end to this if no one else will, Ventry promised himself. And I've got the tools to do it.

He slipped the carefully wrapped gun rig from his knapsack, unfolded its oiled covering, and withdrew his grandfather's long-barreled frontier Colt from its worn leather holster. The gun was a family treasure. Its bone handle was cracked and yellowed by the years, but the old Colt was still in perfect firing order. His granddaddy had worn this rig, had defended his mine on the Comstock against claim jumpers with this gun. It was fitting and proper that it be used on the man who'd killed Amy.

Night was settling over Bitterroot. The fiery orange disc of sun had dropped below the Little Belt Mountains, and the sky was gray slate along the horizon.

Time to strap on the gun. Time to get ready for the train.

It's coming tonight! Lord God, I can feel it out there in the gathering dark, thrumming the rails. I can feel it in my blood and bones.

Well, then, come ahead, god damn you, whoever you are.

I'm ready for you.

Ten p.m. Eleven. Midnight.

It came at midnight.

Rushing toward Bitterroot, clattering in fierce-wheeled thunder, its black bulk sliding over the track in the ash-dark Montana night like an immense, segmented snake—with a single yellow eye probing the terrain ahead.

Ventry heard it long before he saw it. The rails sang

and vibrated around him as he stood tall and resolute in mid-track, a three-cell silver flashlight in his right hand, his heavy sheepskin coat buttoned over the gun at his belt.

Have to flag it down. With the depot closed it won't make a stop. No passengers. It's looking for live game, and it doesn't figure on finding any here at Bitterrroot.

Surprise! *I'm* here. *I'm* alive. Like Amy. Like all the others. Man alone at night. Needs a ride. Climb aboard, pardner. Make yourself to home. Drink? Somethin' to eat? What's your pleasure?

My pleasure is your death—and the death of your freak train, mister! *That's* my pleasure.

It was in sight now, coming fast, slicing a bright round hole in the night—and its sweeping locomotive beam splashed Paul Ventry's body with a pale luminescence.

The rancher swung his flash up, then down, in a high arc. Again. And again.

Stop, you bastard!

*Stop!*

The train began slowing.

Sparks showered from the massive driving wheels as the train reduced speed. Slowing…slower…steel shrieking against steel. An easing of primal force.

It was almost upon him.

Like a great shining insect, the locomotive towered high and black over Ventry, its tall stack shutting out the stars. The rusted tip of the train's thrusting metal cowcatcher gently nudged the toe of his right boot as the incredible night mammoth slid to a final grinding stop.

Now the train was utterly motionless, breathing its white steam into the cold dark, waiting for him as he had waited for it.

Ventry felt a surge of exultation fire his body. He'd been right! It was here—and he was prepared to destroy it, to avenge his sister. It was his destiny. He felt no fear, only a cool and certain confidence in his ability to kill.

A movement at the corner of his eye. Someone was waving to him from the far end of the train, from the last coach, the train's only source of light. All the other passenger cars were dark and blind-windowed; only the last car glowed hazy yellow.

Ventry eased around the breathing locomotive, his boots crunching loudly in the cindered gravel as he moved over the roadbed.

He glanced up at the locomotive's high, double-windowed cabin, but the engineer was lost behind opaque, soot-colored glass. Ventry kept moving steadily forward, toward the distant figure, passing along the linked row of silent, lightless passenger cars. The train bore no marking; it was a uniform, unbroken black.

Ventry squinted at the beckoning figure. Was it the killer himself, surprised and delighted at finding another passenger at this deserted night station?

He slipped the flash into his shoulder knapsack, and eased a hand inside his coat, gripping the warm bone handle of the Colt at his waist. You've had one surprise tonight, mister. Get ready for another.

The, abruptly, he stopped, heart pounding. Ventry recognized the beckoning figure. Impossible! An illusion. Just *couldn't* be. Yet there she was, smiling, waving to him.

"Amy!" Ventry rushed toward his sister in a stumbling run.

But she was no longer in sight when he reached the dimly illumined car. Anxiously, he peered into one of the smoke-yellowed windows. A figure moved hazily inside.

"Amy!" He shouted her name again, mounting the coach steps.

The moment Ventry's boots touched the car's upper platform the train jolted into life. Ventry was thrown to his knees as the coach lurched violently forward.

The locomotive's big driving wheels sparked against steel, gaining a solid grip on the rails as the train surged powerfully from Bitterroot Station.

As Paul Ventry entered the coach, the door snap-locked behind him. Remote-control device. *To make sure I won't leave by the rear exit.* No matter. He'd expected that. He could get out when he had to, when he was ready. He'd come prepared for whatever this madman had in mind.

But Ventry had not been prepared for the emotional shock of seeing Amy. Had he *really* seen her? *Was* it his sister?

No. Of course not. He'd been tricked by his subconscious mind. The fault was his. A lapse in concentration, in judgment.

But *someone* had waved to him—a young girl who looked, at first sight, amazingly like his dead sister.

Where was she now?

And just where was the human devil who ran this train?

Ventry was alone in the car.

To either side of the aisle the rows of richly upholstered green velvet seats were empty. A pair of ornate, scrolled gas lamps, mounted above the arched doorway, cast flickering shadows over antique brass fittings and a handcarved wood ceiling. Green brocade draped the windows.

He didn't know much about trains, but Ventry knew this one *had* to be pre-1900. And probably restored by the rich freak who owned it. Plush was the word.

Well, it was making its last run; Ventry would see to that.

He pulled the flash from his shoulder pack, snapping on the bright beam as he moved warily forward.

The flashlight proved unnecessary. As Ventry entered the second car (doors unlocked; *guess he doesn't mind my going forward*) the over head gas lamps sputtered to life, spreading their pale yellow illumination over the length of the coach.

Again, the plush velvet seats were empty. Except for one. The last seat at the far end of the car. A woman was sitting there, stiff and motionless in the dim light, her back to Ventry.

As he moved toward her, she turned slowly to face him.

By Christ, it *was* Amy!

Paul Ventry rushed to her, sudden tears stinging his eyes. Fiercely, he embraced his sister; she was warm and solid in his arms. "Oh, Sis, I'm so glad you're *alive!*"

But there was no sound from her lips. No words. No emotion. She was rigid in his embrace.

Ventry stepped away from her. "What's wrong? I don't understand why you—"

His words were choked off. Amy had leaped from the seat, cat-quick, to fasten long pale fingers around his throat. Her thumbs dug like sharp spikes into the flesh of Ventry's neck.

He reeled back, gasping for breath, clawing at the incredibly strong hands. He couldn't break her grip.

Amy's face was changing. The flesh was falling away in gummy wet ribbons, revealing raw white bone! In the deep sockets of Amy's grinning skull her eyes were hot red points of fire.

Ventry's right hand found the butt of the Colt, and he dragged the gun free of its holster. Swinging the barrel toward Amy, he fired fiercely into the melting horror of her face.

His bullets drilled round, charred holes in the grinning skull, but Amy's fingers—now all raw bone and slick gristle—maintained their death grip at his throat.

*Axe! Use the axe!*

In a swimming red haze, Ventry snapped the short-handled woodsman's axe free of his belt. And swung it sharply downward, neatly removing Amy's head at shoulder level. The cleanly severed skull rolled into the aisle at his feet.

Yet, horribly, the bony fingers increased their deadly pressure.

Ventry's sight blurred; the coach wavered. As the last

of his oxygen was cut off, he was on the verge of blacking out.

Desperately, he swung the blade again, missing the Amy-thing entirely. The axe buried itself in thick green velvet.

The train thrashed; its whistle shrieked wildly in the rushing night, a cry of pain—and the seat rippled in agony. Oily black liquid squirted from the sliced velvet.

At Ventry's throat, the bony fingers dropped away.

In numbed shock, he watched his sister's rotting corpse flow down into the seat, melting and mixing with the central train body, bubbling wetly...

*Oh, sweet Jesus! Everything's moving! The whole foul train is alive!*

And Ventry accepted it. Sick with horror and revulsion, he accepted it. He was a realist, and this thing was real. No fantasy. No dream.

Real.

Which meant he had to kill it. Not the man who owned it, because such a man did not exist. Somehow, the train itself, ancient and rusting in the high mountains, had taken on a sentient life of its own. The molecular components of iron and wood and steel had, over a slow century, transformed themselves into living tissue—and this dark hell-thing had rolled out onto the Montana plains seeking food, seeking flesh to sustain it, sleeping, sated, through the frozen winters, hibernating, then stirring to hungry life again as the greening earth renewed itself.

*Lot of strange things in the Little Belt.*

Don't think about it, Ventry warned himself. Just do what you came to do: Kill it! Kill the foul thing. Blow it out of existence!

He carried three explosive charges in his knapsack, each equipped with a timing device. All right, make your plan! Set one here at the end of the train, another in the middle coach, and plant the final charge in the forward car.

No good. If the thing had the power to animate its

dead victims, it also had the power to fling off his explosive devices, to rid itself of them as a dog shakes leaves from its coat.

I'll have to go after it the way you go after a snake; to kill a snake, you cut off its head.

So go for the brain.

Go for the engine.

The train had left the main rail system now, and was on a rusted spur track, climbing steeply into the Little Belt range.

It was taking Ventry into the high mountains. One last meal of warm flesh, then the long winter's sleep.

The train was going home.

Three cars to go.

Axe in hand, Ventry was moving steadily toward the engine, through vacant, gas-lit coaches, wondering how and when it would attack him again.

Did it know he meant to kill it? Possibly it had no fear of him. God knows it was strong. And no human had ever harmed it in the past. Does the snake fear the mouse?

Maybe it would leave him alone to do his work; maybe it didn't realize how lethal this mouse could be.

But Ventry was wrong.

Swaying in the clattering rush of the train, he was halfway down the aisle of the final coach when the tissue around him rippled into motion. Viscid black bubbles formed on the ceiling of the car, and in the seats. Growing. Quivering. Multiplying.

One by one, the loathsome globes swelled and burst—giving birth to a host of nightmare figures. Young and old. Man, woman, child. Eyes red and angry.

They closed on Ventry in the clicking interior of the hell coach, moving toward him in a rotting tide.

He had seen photos of many of them in the Lewiston library. Vanished passengers, like Amy, devoured and ab-

sorbed and now regenerated as fetid ectoplasmic horrors—
literal extensions of the train itself.

Ventry knew that he was powerless to stop them. The
Amy-thing had proven that.

But he still had the axe, and a few vital seconds before
the train-things reached him.

Ventry swung the razored blade left and right, slashing brutally at seat and floor, cutting deep with each swift
blow. Fluid gushed from a dozen gaping wounds, a rubbery
mass of coil-like innards, like spilled guts, erupted from the
seat to Ventry's right, splashing him with gore.

The train screamed into the Montana night, howling
like a wounded beast.

The passenger-things lost form, melting into the aisle.

Now Ventry was at the final door, leading to the coal
car directly behind the engine.

It was locked against him.

The train had reached its destination at the top of the
spur, was rolling down a side track leading to a deserted
mine. Its home. Its cave. Its dark hiding place.

The train would feast now.

Paul Ventry used the last of his strength on the door.
Hacking at it. Slashing wildly. Cutting his way through.

Free! In a freezing blast of night wind, Ventry
scrambled across the coal tender toward the shining black
locomotive.

And reached it.

A heavy, gelatinous membrane separated him from the
control cabin. The membrane pulsed with veined life.

Got to get inside…reach the brain of the thing…

Ventry drove the blade deep, splitting the veined skin.
And burst through into the cabin.

Its interior was a shock to Ventry's senses; he was as-
sailed by a stench so powerful that bile rushed into his throat.
He fought back a rising nausea.

Brass and wood and iron had become throbbing flesh. Levers and controls and pressure gauges were coated with a thick, crawling slime. The roof and sides of the cabin were moving.

A huge, red, heart-like mass pulsed and shimmered wetly in the center of the cabin, its sickly crimson glow illuminating his face.

He did not hesitate.

Ventry reached into the knapsack, pulled out an explosive charge, and set the device for manual. All he needed to do was press a metal switch, toss the charge at the heart-thing, and jump from the cabin.

It was over. He'd won!

But before he could act, the entire chamber heaved up in a bubbled, convulsing pincer movement, trapping Ventry like a fly in a web.

He writhed in the jellied grip of the train-thing. The explosive device had been jarred from his grasp. The axe, too, was lost in the mass of crushing slime-tissue.

Ventry felt sharp pain fire along his back. *Teeth!* The thing had sprouted rows of needled teeth and was starting to eat him alive!

The knapsack; he was still wearing it!

Gasping, dizzy with pain, Ventry plunged his right hand into the sack, closing bloodied fingers around the second explosive device. Pulled it loose, set it ticking.

*Sixty seconds.*

If he could not fight free in that space of time he'd go up with the train. A far better way to die than being ripped apart and devoured. Death would be a welcome release.

Incredibly, the train-thing seemed to *know* that its life was in jeopardy. Its shocked tissues drew back, cringing away from the ticking explosive charge.

Ventry fell to his knees on the slimed floor.

*Thirty seconds.*

He saw the sudden gleam of rails to his right, just below him, and he launched himself in a plunging dive through the severed membrane.

Struck ground. Searing pain. Right shoulder. Broken bone.

Hell with it! *Move, damn you, move!*

Ventry rolled over on his stomach, pain lacing his body. Pushed himself up. Standing now.

*Five seconds.*

Ventry sprawled forward. Legs won't support me!

Then *crawl!*

Into heavy brush. Still crawling—dragging his lacerated, slime-smeared body toward a covering of rocks.

Faster! No more time…Too late!

The night became sudden day.

The explosion picked up Ventry and tossed him into the rocks like a boneless doll.

The train-thing screamed in a whistling death-agony as the concussion sundered it, scattering its parts like wet confetti over the terrain.

Gobbets of bleeding tissue rained down on Ventry as he lay in the rocks. But through the pain and the stench and the nausea his lips were curved into a thin smile.

He was unconscious when the Montana sun rose that morning, but when Sheriff John Longbow arrived on the scene he found Paul Ventry alive.

Alive and triumphant.

I was quite pleased by the critical reaction to this story. Writer Joe Lansdale praised it as "a masterpiece." When I faced the prospect of writing my first horror novel, I decided to combine this story with one called "The Cure" (about a serial killer). I added new material on sheep ranching, told the reader much more about the Ventry family, and had Ventry's adult son destroy the train after the father is killed trying to avenge his daughter's (rather than his sister's) death. I greatly expanded the serial killer story by having him roam through Montana, strangling selected victims en route, until he finally encounters the Ventrys and the train. In effect, two novels in one.

The result was *Helltracks*, published by Cemetery Dance Publications in hardcover and Avon in paperback.

I am proud of this story, which would not exist had I not, one night, experienced a very unsettling dream.

# THIRTEEN 13

## HOMING IN ON YOUR HOMETOWN:
### YOUR ORIGINS ARE UNIQUE

Several beginning writers have told me, sadly, that they would write more if only they had a real subject. "I just don't have anything to write about," they declare.

Wrong. You, as a beginning writer, have at least one great subject to write about: your own hometown.

Too many writers feel that the town they grew up in is of no literary consequence. Not nearly exotic or interesting enough. They think, if I'd just grown up in Honolulu, London, or Cape Town...

The truth is, they're blinding themselves to the richness of their past. The smallest town in North America (or anywhere on the planet) is well worth writing about.

I grew up in Kansas City and have effectively utilized my Missouri background in many of my published stories and scripts. I have a special knowledge of Kansas City, unique things to say about it, and original observations about the life, the culture, and the people. (Producer/director Dan Curtis used to tell me I wrote "the best crackers in the industry" an unintended gift to me from many of the adults I knew during my youth.)

Go back to your roots. Where did you grow up? Tell your readers about the singular landscape you already possess in your memory. Put your town into a short story or novel. No one knows more about it than you do, and no one has your perspective, so put that unique knowledge to solid use.

Ray Bradbury made a career out of writing about his hometown, from *Dandelion Wine* to *The Martian Chronicles*. (His "Mars" is simply a transposed version of Waukegan, Illinois.)

Hemingway's "Nick Adams" stories are really all about young Ernest in northern Michigan.

And regardless of where they were supposed to have taken place, Max Brand wrote endless stories about ranch life in California's San Joaquin Valley, which he knew intimately from his hardscrabble youth.

But, let's say, you grew up in Los Angeles or San Francisco. "Well," you moan. "Look at all the books written about these cities. There's nothing left for me to write about."

Wrong. Each of us has our own unique take on our hometown.

Although a native of Baltimore, Dashiell Hammett saw his adopted city of San Francisco through *his* eyes—as a corrupt city—and wrote about it from that viewpoint. But if *you* grew up there, you would very likely have a completely different perspective.

Put your town, the town that only *you* know on paper as a background for your protagonist. Let the character see and react to San Francisco (or wherever) as you once did.

Material for a novel? Material for several novels—and each one a book that only you can write.

# FOURTEEN 14

## WHERE IDEAS COME FROM:
## AND HOW TO KEEP THEM COMING

I've been asked countless times, "Mr. Nolan, where do you get your ideas?"

Ideas come from everywhere, from:
- newspaper stories
- overheard conversations. Sit at the counter of a neighborhood restaurant and *listen* to people
- historical events
- magazine articles
- TV news
- surfing the Internet
- trips (across your neighborhood or across the world)
- childhood memories (a rich seedbed)
- family experiences (your spouse, and your children, all have—or will lead you to—ideas)
- reading other writers
- from dreams (which I have already discussed).

If you keep an open mind, and actively observe the world around you, the ideas will keep arriving. Most professional writers I know have far more ideas than they can get onto paper.

For me, the most productive period of the day is in the early morning "twilight zone," just before full awareness, when my brain is totally relaxed. It is then that my subconscious has the opportunity to express itself.

Be aware of the life that goes on around you. Trust your subconscious, and you will discover that you have within you a limitless store-house of ideas just waiting to be discovered.

# FIFTEEN 15

## THOSE GOLDEN NOTEBOOKS: NEVER LEAVE HOME WITHOUT ONE

Personal notebooks are an essential for every writer. Because notebook pages are capable of recording the fresh inner life of your consciousness, over time they evolve into a literary gold mine which can be worked throughout your career, offering you an endless supply of story and novel ideas.

Since 1963 I have filled nine (8½- by 11-inch) notebooks. Nearly a thousand pages of personal notes. You may prefer smaller, pocket-sized notebooks, or maybe three-ring binders, for your notes—whatever works best for you. However, I strongly caution you to make and keep your notes on paper. Although a variety of electronic recordkeeping possibilities exist today, technology moves so swiftly that these machines become obsolete at increasingly faster rates. Making audio notes on electronic equipment is guaranteed to render your notes unavailable to you in just a few years; while notes made on paper will be instantly accessible for all the rest of your life. Your notebooks are one of your most important career assets, so make sure you make those notes on paper.

What should go into your notebooks? That's up to you, but here is what has gone into mine:
- plot ideas
- overheard (and imaginary) conversations
- descriptions (of people, places, things)
- personal philosophy and observations
- story or book titles

- travel notes
- lists (of all kinds)
- capsule reviews of books and films
- research data
- dialogue (real, dreamt, and imagined)
- scenes (real, and for projected stories)
- statistics and odd facts
- verse
- childhood memories
- odd names
- loves and hates
- anecdotes
- critical opinions
- character sketches
- notes taken from TV, newspapers, magazines, and
the Internet.

Think of notebooks as your writing collaborators. The material you put into your notebooks will often reappear later, in your fiction. Notes and plot ideas become stories. A particular exchange of dialogue may suit one of your future characters. That bizarre fact, anecdote, or bit of research data may be just the thing you need to complete a scene or spur a new story.

And there's no censorship. You are free to record anything of value to *you*—knowing that you will not be judged by the words because no one but you will have access to them.

Take a notebook with you, wherever you go: to work, to the library or bookstore, to dinners and films, and on trips and vacations. Keeping a notebook with you should become as natural as carrying a wallet, purse, or backpack. You never know when you have to capture an important thought or emotion on paper. But record these *immediately*. Otherwise, such fragments will almost certainly be lost to you forever.

Here's a group of sample entries, randomly selected from my notebooks, to give you an idea of what you might want to put in yours:

The trouble with the young nightclub stripper in New

Orleans was simple: Her feet were dirty.

The writer had an editor's head (with pipe and horn rims) mounted over the fireplace, a stuffed publisher in the den, and an agent-skin rug on the floor.

Remembering the healthy way the children looked in Paris, as if their cheeks had been rouged…like fresh peaches.

After a day spent with the poetry of Robert Frost, he felt the seasons in his blood and bones…snow and flowers and rain were on the pages.

He was close to insane, a man toe-dancing on the pin-head of reality.

An old man talking. Territorial Prison. Yuma, Arizona: "They threw me inta the hell hole at Yuma. Terrible place. By day, hot enough to make the Devil sweat. Freezin' cold at night—and with us sleepin' in open iron bunks with one thin blanket a'tween you and pneumonia. I whupped a guard, an' they shackled me inta the snake pit. Cut outa solid rock. They'd throw in rattlers an' scorpions, but I *et* 'em. Knew how to snap off a rattler's head. Handled 'em like a muleskinner handles a bullwhip. Trick with a scorpion is watchin' you don't get tail-bit. I et 'em raw, after twistin' off their tails. Hell, I could see in the dark like a goddam owl. Escape from Yuma was near impossible. No roads in, back then. Just river an' rail. Big paddle boats down the Colorado, with armed guards on deck. Open desert all around. If you swum the river, an' survived the current, the damn Injuns, they'd track ya down for a fifty-dollar bounty, dead or alive. But, by Jasper, I made it out clean. Lost a couple'a fingers. Smashed up my right leg—but I sure as hell made it out. An' I'm the only man livin' can say the same."

"It's like when a bishop farts during High Mass," said

the Irish bartender. "You know it's possible, but you sure don't *expect* it."

A good writer has three eyes. Two in his head, and one in his heart.

He took her to the Sta-Pure Motel in Intercourse, Pennsylvania.

"You know something " the man said to his wife. "I'm just *not* a perceptive person. All my life, from childhood, I've been a totally *un*perceptive person. Tonight, lying here in bed, I just realized the truth about myself." "I think that's very perceptive," his wife said.

A fat man with tiny feet and the face of a spoiled baby.

"I feel that my walking dead man who needs blood from young virgins has more depth of character than *your* walking dead man who needs blood from young virgins," said one TV horror writer to another.

Fact: The brain can store 600 memories per second. There are ten billion neurons in the human brain, each actively in communication via hundreds of routes. Every moment of our life is stored in our brain: every color, every sound, every spoken word, all stored and recorded. [This is a notebook entry I made some years ago. The facts of human physiology, as currently known to science, are somewhat different now which is a warning to writers: Be constantly on the alert for the changes that take place, as scientific discoveries and historical knowledge continue to expand at ever-increasing rates.]

She stared at him with emotionless eyes as though a steady rain inside her body had put out the fire of her personality.

Batman story idea: What if Robin falls in love with someone who turns out to be the Joker's daughter? [I wrote and sold this as "Daddy's Girl."]

Rejection letter: "We are herewith returning your leg. Thank you for sending it along to us, but we must regretfully decline it. Although it seems to work fine (the toes especially appealed to us), we have an overstock of legs at present. However, we are always in the market for good ears and fingers, should you care to submit along those lines."

"It's funny how people feel about people who are funny."

"I don't get you."

"Well, you're a funny guy, right?"

"I guess so. I guess I *am* funny."

"Well, I get a funny feeling about a funny guy like you. There's something funny about a guy who's always funny. Do you know what I'm talking about?"

"Sure, but I find that funny."

"I can't go on talking to you."

"Why not?"

"Because the word 'funny' has lost all meaning for me."

"Gee, that's funny."

Rhythm is everything in writing. A writer's rhythm is his or her style.

It was one of those nameless, off-the-road cafes where even the flies move lazily, sated and undisturbed in the dim, smoky-yellow interior. You order "just coffee" because, although you're hungry, coffee is the only thing you're willing to risk in such a place. You note, with a slight grimace, that your water glass is clouded with the same residue of grease which permeates the air you breathe. The cook who serves you wears a stained butcher's apron, and you decide not to look at his hands.

You can store up hate, but love always spills out.

[After reading *Timebends*, by Arthur Miller]: Miller's life story pressed many buttons of memory in his own life, and despite their difference in age (Miller, seventy-two, born in 1915), they shared many things: the old, horse-drawn ice wagons with the cake of melting crystal slung over the iceman's gunny-sacked shoulder, held by silver pincers, the man smelling of wet leather and canvas... the noisy, always-welcome arrival of the coal truck in winter, grinding along our driveway to disgorge its tumble of black coal down the racketing tin chute into our basement...the warm satisfaction of standing in front of the heaped coal, fresh-dumped and glittery-dark in the damp basement, knowing that we had winter heat... carnival-colored penny candy in a giant glass globe on the drugstore shelf...the freedom of a bicycle, wheels waiting to take you to magic weekend places far from your home streets—all shared memories, brought sharply back into the light by Miller's graceful, affecting prose.

He walked always with his head down, as though life itself had a low-beam ceiling.

Fact [1987]: 23 million people in the U.S. are functionally illiterate (13% of the population), and 35 million more are semi-literate (not able to read beyond an eighth-grade level). Together, they total 58 million (of 240 million people in the U.S.), nearly 25% of the population. In the *world* (with a global population of five billion), there are 250,000 new babies born each day.

Driving out of New York City through the long Holland Tunnel, leaving the great stone circus behind.

Story idea: Roadside diner. Bearded guy mumbling at the counter. Angry. He was stopped by the Highway Patrol. Starts talking to another weirdo at the counter (baseball cap, sunglasses, bare-arm tattoos). Offers second weirdo a ride. They leave. What happens when these two misfits are together on a dark road in the bearded guy's car? Do they plan a robbery together? Does the second weirdo try to kill the first weirdo? Steal his car? Are they both *really* crazy? Do they end up killing each other? Or kidnapping someone? Or what?

On the production set in Canada: Stage mother to child actor, age nine: "Now go ahead and apologize to Mr. Nolan for not getting all of his dialogue right."

Sleep is a form of insanity. You have no control over your mind; it can take you anywhere, do *anything* with you.

In 400 B.C.E. the Greek philosopher Democritus declared: "Much is perceptible which is not perceived by us."

He was a large man with a small soul.

The silence of Death Valley Junction: so quiet, you can hear a mule bray clear across town, with the stars (a million suns) frozen in spangled solitude above the night desert.

The loss of a close friend is more than a shock, it's a small advance on your own death. A dead friend carries part of *your* past to *his* grave.

"Tellya a secret. Most writers are cold bastards, afraid of emotion," the hack said, as he gently patted his red hairpiece. "Me, I'm not afraid of emotion. I use real deep human emotion in my scripts. That's what I'm known for, my specialty. I'm not afraid to cry on paper."

Ten favorite horror films of the '30s:
*Dracula* (1930)
*Frankenstein* (1931)
*Island of Lost Souls* (1932)
*King Kong* (1933)
*The Bride of Frankenstein* (1935)
*The Black Room* (1935)
*The Walking Dead* (1936)
*The Invisible Ray* (1936)
*The Wizard of Oz* (1939)
*The Hound of the Baskervilles* (1939)

"I visited the book," he said, "but I didn't want to *live* in it. I'm not strong enough to exist inside such oppressive fictional houses."

The killer shark: unchanged for 350 million years!

Title for a horror story: "The Stone Ghost"

"You really write good," the woman told him.
"Thank you."
"My boy writes awful. He's over twenty, and he just writes awful."
"That's too bad."
"Writes just like he did in grade school. Oh, you can *read* the words, but they look just awful."
"Then you're talking about *hand*writing?"
She looked confused. "What other kind *is* there?"

The bumping, stumble-footed, aimless walk of a two-year-old.

Fact [1990]: There are 100 billion atoms in one molecule of DNA—the same as the number of suns in a typical galaxy.

On the set of *Star Trek*: "Aren't you supposed to die this afternoon?" asked the first actor.

"Nope, I'll die tomorrow," replied the second actor.

Dream poem (composed in sleep):
    In the shelled
    winding sheet
    of her turtled nightmares
    she sand-crawled
    the hallways of madness.

The old are not always wise; sometimes they are just old.

The gun spat, like grease on a hot skillet, and the big guy learned how to die in one easy lesson.

Nostalgia begins with maturity. Age has nothing to do with it.

Dream (often repeated): He was flying over the street, above the heads of the walking people, none of whom knew he was up there. He found that he could also jump over houses, but he had to watch out for the telephone wires. Flying, for him, was incredibly simple. He was amazed that others found it so difficult, or even impossible.

"How old is the Earth?"

"All grown up, I'd say. Four billion years old, give or take a billion."

"Wow, it's no kid, is it?"

"It knows its way around the sun, all right."

Names:
    Jerry Atrics
    Mal Feasance

Jenny Talia
Eggs Benedict
Ben Dover

A Shakespearean scholar's license plate:
2B R NT 2B

The Haunted Castle in Hollywood: big rope web, complete with spider…wax figures…female dancers with glow-in-the-dark tassels on their breasts…Ski shop: white rocks for snow in window…couple on skis, heavy-sweatered and mittened in the hot sun…

Population growth: In 1700: the eastern colonies had 262,000 European residents (others probably not counted).

In 1800: five and a half million residents were counted (often not including non-Caucasians such as American Indians, while non-Caucasians of African or Asian descent were often either ignored completely or counted individually as some fractional part of a whole person).

In 1900 (when my mother was six): U.S. population was 76 million.

In 1930: almost 123 million.

In 1940: over 131 million.

In 1960: 178½ million.

In 1988: 245 million (doubled since 1930).

He felt faintly sick from too many coffees, and from the iced Scotch he'd had in the lounge car. Now, sitting by the window in the effortless rush of the train, he listened to the adding-machine click of wheels and thought about all the strangers living out there in that dark, alien night country beyond the glass.

Hills like folded brown buffalo robes.

Bumper sticker: MICE IS NICE.

She waited for him to seduce her, and he waited for her to seduce him—so no one got seduced.

It was a crazy, mottled sky out of Jackson Pollack.

Scene for a projected historical:

He was a stalwart, thick-shouldered fellow with a flowing sweep of moustache, dressed in the finery of a typical Spanish cavalier. A large ruby ring flashed fire from his right hand, which rested lightly on the chased-gold hilt of a cut-and-thrust rapier. His cape was of black velvet, worked with silver, and a plumed feather swept up from the crown of his wide-brimmed hat.

"Will you have ale with me, sir?" he asked.

"I don't drink with Spanish dogs," I said quietly.

"Oddsblood!" His face flushed hotly. "You're English! A swine of an Englishman!"

"I serve my king, Charles Stuart."

"You'll serve the point of my blade for your arrogance!" he roared, as he smashed aside the tankard of ale and stepped back quickly. The heavy rapier glittered in his hand. "Damn me, if I won't spit you like a roasting pig."

By then my own weapon had hissed free of its scabbard, a short sword of fine English steel. I danced back as he lunged at me. Then, with a strong forward thrust, I drove my blade solidly into the deep hollow of his throat. Pulled free, my sword ran crimson with Spanish blood. The lace of his high collar rapidly darkened from an outpouring of his life's fluid, and with a choked death rattle he crashed forward and down to the tavern floor.

"This job is okay," the waitress told him, "except for the midnight-to-seven shift. That's when you get all the lousy drunks."

"They give you a lot of trouble, huh?"

"They make me hate people. No kidding, after a week of waiting on lousy drunks, I go around hating the human race. That's why I got off the late shift."

"Do you like people in the daytime?"

"*Love* 'em," she said.

A Paris moon the color of vintage wine…the dark, green-black rain forests of Belgium…

Gulls plied the air like pirates, ranging the coast in scattered gray battalions.

"Sir, you are a blatherskite, a cutpurse, a lickspittle, a dizzard, a dunderpate, and a jabbernowl."

The smell was strong enough to gag a maggot.

Under the old Hollywood system: F. Scott Fitz-gerald was one of a total of thirty-one writers who worked on the film of *A Yank at Oxford*. (Eight writers received final screen credit.)

The midnight wounds
   gape
   open-mouths
   in the flesh of darkness.

She was convinced, utterly and calmly convinced, that the potatoes were watching her. "They *all* have eyes, you know," she told me.

Story idea: "The Man Who Was Billy"

I watched as Billy shot the old man. You sadistic little shit, I thought. You *enjoyed* that.

[A contemporary man is slowly being transformed. Fascinated with Old West lore. Gradually *becoming* Billy the Kid, a bit more "slippage" each new day. Line between past and present dissolves, and there he is: dirty, unshaven, old bowler hat, ragged clothes…]

At end:

"Billy," I called softly.

He spun toward me.

I shot him.

My name? James P. Garrett. But my friends call me Pat.


The furred slide of phosphor cats through moon-fleshed, birch-white woods...


Opening for a crime tale:

She had luminous blue eyes, honey-gold skin, pouting lips, full and sensuous, and a spill of blazing red hair. Her legs, in black stretch pants, were long and coltish. She knew the effect she had on men. All she had to do was walk into a room and every male eye was on her. She was hot. The drift-ing scent of her perfumed body could stoke a furnace. If you were a man, and she asked, you'd kill for her. That's what started it all. She asked, and I killed. For her. I killed a man because Linda asked me to. It was just that simple.


"I married this businessman-werewolf," Janet told her therapist. "He's always sleeping at night, except when the moon is full, and then he's out in the woods. Me, I'm *al-ways* up at night 'cuz I, you know, sleep all day in my coffin while Joe's at work. He's in the plastering business, so we never—"

"Coffin?"

"Yeah. In the basement. You didn't know I'm a vam-pire?"

"You hadn't mentioned it."

"Well, lemme tellya, vampires should never marry werewolves."

"It *does* present problems," said the therapist.

# SIXTEEN 16

## THE OUTLINE:
### YOUR CREATIVE ROAD MAP

**M**any novice writers have told me (with glee in their tone): "Oh, I never know where my story is going, and I don't *want* to know. I just give my creativity full rein, and then I see what happens next."

This approach to fiction can be detrimental not only to a specific story, but to the habitual working patterns you develop that either support, or do not support, the building of a writing career. When writers work without knowing where their story is going, they all too often become mired in meaningless action, with no idea what to write next.

Writers need to know how to resolve the central conflict of their story or novel, and what the emotional payoff will be. These answers are not achieved by plunging ahead blindly, without regard to content or form.

Am I advising that a written outline is essential? No. Detailed, written outlines (which some beginning writers seem to specialize in) often inhibit creativity. If the writer follows an outline too closely and neglects to leave room for creative freedom—the twists and turns that occur naturally in any narrative—the result will usually be dull and unpublishable.

I do, however, believe in some form of *mental* outline, and this mental outline can indeed be written on paper, along with whatever details the writer feels should be included.

Usually when you begin a road trip, you have a specific destination in mind. Although you may not know exactly where you'll stop for gas and food, and you might not know in advance exactly where you're going to sleep on the nights en route, you will usually have a firm destination in mind, as well as a general idea of the highways you'll use to get there. During your journey, you may impulsively decide to check out a local fair, tourist attraction, or historic site—you might spontaneously exit the interstate so you can take the longer, but much more enjoyable, scenic route around the lake.

But ideally, you should begin your trip knowing what your main challenges are likely to be (such as a predicted late spring snowstorm through California's Sierra Nevada mountains), how you will likely deal with the probable challenges you expect to face, and—most important—where you're going to end up.

As a writer, you need to know your destination—and particularly with novels.

Short stories and novels are different. My method in writing short fiction is fairly consistent: I first get the idea, along with an opening. Then, at that same time, I create a mental picture of the ending usually with the final line of the story forming itself in my head. For shorter fiction, these story points are what my (usually unwritten) *outline* consists of.

For a novel, however, a written outline, which does *not* have to be rigidly followed, can prove to be of great assistance in keeping you on track, functioning as a road map for your fictional journey. But it should be flexible, so that unplanned situations, characters, and plot developments can be included as they occur.

For the more complex fictional works—novels and novellas— my usual method is to jot down ideas for scenes, turning points, and characters (sometimes with relevant dialogue) on a series of index cards, which I later arrange in sequence to form my dramatic arc. This method is similar to that of a film director who, prior to production, storyboards his film. The cards give the creator a basic path to follow—but always allow for creative flexibility.

As a beginning writer, try several methods, whatever comes to your mind, until you find the ones that work best for you. Regardless of your choice, though, always leave space for your imagination to flourish and for surprises to happen—as well as for that mystical experience when you dip into the well of self for treasures previously unsuspected and unknown.

# SEVENTEEN 17

## THE IMPORTANCE OF RESEARCH:
### YOUR ESSENTIAL DETAILS MUST BE ACCURATE

Hemingway declared: "Write what you know." I would extend this to: "Write what you know—or what you can find out about."

Almost everything I've written over the five decades of my career has involved research—a basic tool for any writer. When I began to research my writing subjects, there was no Internet. I had to depend on bookstores, magazine shops, and libraries—public, university, and government. Today, writers can search the Web and find practically everything they need to know on any subject, all without having to leave their computer.

However, be warned: Much of the "information" available on the Internet is erroneous, either intentionally or by mistake. Double- and triple-check any "facts" you've obtained before using them in your writing, preferably by verifying them with expert, non-Internet sources. If you want to create and maintain a professional reputation, make certain your "facts" are *factual* before you submit any creative work to an agent or editor.

Research provides essential details. If you're going to set a story or a novel in Southern California, you need to know which trees grow there, which flowers are in bloom in which seasons, the styles and periods of architecture, the layout of the freeways, and much more. For example, *June gloom* (the days in late May and early June when, because of the nearness of the Pacific Ocean, Southern California residents wake up to cool, foggy, and often depressing overcast...which then burns off into bright sunshine by midday).

If you are researching a truly complex subject and are having difficulty understanding it, go to the children's or young adult section of your local bookstore or library and find books that deal with that subject. You'll get the information you need in a simple, clear, and easy-to-understand form.

In my novel *Helltracks*, Josh Ventry, my protagonist, works for his father on the family's Montana sheep ranch. In order to achieve a realistic background, I did considerable research on sheep ranching. When I began, I knew absolutely *nothing* about sheep beyond the fact that they bleated and were woolly, but by the time I sat down to write my novel, I'd learned what I needed to know. I was able to put this newly gained knowledge to excellent use in my narrative.

In researching a character's background, you'll probably end up with a lot more information than your story requires. You must then select what fits and what doesn't. (The extra material might end up in another of your short stories or novels down the line, so save your research notes.)

When Charles Dickens wrote about the horrors of a London childhood in *Oliver Twist*, he didn't have to research the period since he had lived it. However, if *you* decided to set a novel in nineteenth-century London, you'd have to do in-depth research to depict the era.

Kathleen Winsor offers a case in point: In 2000, when the Chicago Review Press reissued *Forever Amber*, Winsor's romantic period novel, Barbara Taylor Bradford contributed a new introduction in which she wrote:

> What struck me most forcibly was the enormous amount of research the author had done. ...When Kathleen Winsor was married to...Robert Herwig, she became fascinated by the books he was then reading for his college theme on Charles II. She began to read them as well, and went on reading books about this period for the next five years. After that, she wrote the novel. ...She created a marvelous sense of time and place and atmosphere, and it is this that sets the tone of the novel. ...I once described fiction as a monumental lie that has to have the absolute ring of truth if it is to succeed. And that ring of truth invariably comes from

research, which gives a novel its authenticity.

My "Black Mask Boys" trilogy of novels, set in 1930s Hollywood, is another case in point. I mixed history with fiction and featured Dashiell Hammett, Raymond Chandler, and Erle Stanley Gardner as amateur detectives who solve fictional crimes I invented for them. I did massive research on the lives of these three real-life characters and on the period in which they lived. (I was immensely gratified when mystery master Robert B. Parker commented on my work, stating that it "masterfully penetrates the surreal *Black Mask* world of Southern California in the 1930s. Nolan has captured the essence of both an era and a literary form in one brilliant exercise.")

Without extensive research this would not have been possible.

In a piece I wrote for the *Los Angeles Times*, I gave a negative review of a science fiction anthology which was full of errors. The editor clearly had not done his research, and had depended on his faulty memory for various titles and facts. He got many of them wrong, and I called him on it.

The publisher was blameless. Publishers assume that writers do their research before projects are completed. I was able to spot the errors in this particular anthology because I was quite familiar with the purported "facts" under discussion.

If you do not do the proper research, you will be called on it—and often publicly. There is no excuse for factual errors which could easily have been avoided.

As a writer, the facts are your responsibility.

Make certain that what you write is factually correct.

# EIGHTEEN 18

## HOW IS THE WEATHER?
### NATURAL SETTINGS ADD VIGOR

Weather surrounds and enfolds every story or novel. Each tale takes place in calm or storm, under clear or cloudy skies, in rain or shine. Weather plays an important role in fiction, because it can not only strongly affect the mood of your story, it can also be a natural impetus for character change and plot development.

In *The Shining*, Stephen King uses heavy snow to isolate his characters at the Overlook Hotel. The severe weather cuts them off from outside help.

Hemingway's Frederic Henry, in *A Farewell to Arms*, walks back to his hotel in the rain after witnessing the death of the woman he loved. Sunlight would not have served the mood of this scene.

A burning sun was perfect, however, to dramatize the trials of the vast desert crossing in *Lawrence of Arabia*.

A Kansas tornado whisks Dorothy off to a strange land in *The Wizard of Oz*.

In Alfred Hitchcock's *Psycho*, a blinding road-storm forces Janet Leigh to seek shelter at the deadly Bates Motel.

While calm, sweet weather carries its own fictional language (think of new love blooming in the fragrant caress of a soft spring evening), severe weather—with its fires, floods, mudslides, and tidal waves— may be used not just for atmosphere, but to create the kinds of character challenges that result in intense drama.

When you next sit down to write, ask yourself how weather can enhance your story. Be aware of weather—and use it.

# Nineteen 19

## Humor as a Tool:
### Diffusing Intensity

Humor is a primary element of my fiction—particularly in my short stories, which (because of their concentrated brevity) can be intense. I use humor to break the tension and to give my readers some breathing space—a relief from the often-grim fictional events I have created.

In contrast, many contemporary shock-fiction writers present only unrelenting terror, which becomes uncomfortable, and eventually exhausts the reader.

I attempt to avoid such traps by using humor as a tool in my fiction. A few smiles along the way can act as an escape valve, helping to diffuse a story's grim tone of terror.

If you'd like to read what I'm talking about, I refer you to *Dark Universe* and *Nightworlds*, my most recent collections (both in paperback from Leisure Books).

In my story, "One of Those Days," my protagonist has a mental breakdown and goes to see his psychiatrist. The story is told in a breezy, larking style, but the subtext is madness and the loss of control. It ends this way:

> I stared at Dr. Mellowthin.
> "What's the matter?" he asked, somewhat uneasily.
> "Well," I said, "to begin with, you have large brown, sad-looking, liquidy eyes."
> "And…"

"And I bet your nose is cold!" I grinned.

"Anything else?"

"Not really."

"What about my *overall* appearance?"

"Well, of course, you're covered with long black, shaggy hair, even down to the tips of your big floppy ears."

A moment of strained silence.

"Can you do tricks?" I asked.

"A few," Mellowthin replied, shifting in his chair.

"Roll over!" I commanded.

He did.

"Play dead!"

His liquidy eyes rolled up white and his long pink tongue lolled loosely from his jaws.

"Good doggie," I said. "Nice doggie."

"Woof," barked Dr. Mellowthin softly, wagging his tail.

Putting on my homburg, I tossed him a bone I'd saved from the garden and left his office.

There was no getting around it.

This was simply one of those days.


As you, too, will probably discover in your career, the judicious use of humor can be one of the most versatile tools in a writer's basket of skills.

# III.

## CHARACTER DEVELOPMENT

# TWENTY 20

## CHARACTERIZATION WITHIN ACTION:
### ACTIONS SPEAK LOUDER THAN WORDS

I was a young teenager when I began reading the western novels of Max Brand. Naturally at that time, I read his fiction strictly for enjoyment. Only much later, when I was a working professional writer, did I realize that he had taught me a most valuable lesson: Character can be revealed by action.

Brand showed that what a person *does* demonstrates who and what that person *is*.

Many short stories and novels depend on detailed description to build the characters, but this is static (and usually unsatisfactory) writing.

In an action-adventure novel, for example, if you spend a page of description telling your readers *about* your protagonist—rather than allowing your fictional character to reveal him- or herself through that person's actions—the narrative flow is usually broken, and the story generally grinds slowly to a halt.

For most fiction, a good general rule to follow is: Show. Don't tell. (And in scripting, of course, this rule always applies.)

A tip of the sombrero, then, to Max Brand—one of the greatest writing teachers I ever had.

# TWENTY ONE 21

## BUILDING A CHARACTER:
## "WHEREVER YOU GO, THERE YOU ARE."

*Your main character is always you.*

Every character I create—male or female, young or old, from any of the backgrounds I have written about—always contains some part of me.

As a writer, you need a character base upon which to construct your story, and that base is *you*: your experiences, your emotions, and your imagined actions when facing fictional situations.

In *Logan's Run*, I am Logan and I am Jessica. They partake of my fears, my (hoped for) courage under stress, my desire to live and love and survive. In *Helltracks*, I am Josh Ventry as he hunts down the death train.

It cannot be otherwise, since no one is able to write out of a vacuum. We fill in the empty places with bits of ourselves.

But, you ask, what about using real people you've known? What about basing your fictional characters on members of your family, your friends…or your enemies? For instance: that boss you hated in your first office job. Or that adventurous girl you met in college. Your irritating uncle. Can they be portrayed in your fiction?

Yes and no. Sometimes I have the visual image of a real person in mind as I write, but usually this real person is simply a starting point. As the story takes form, I alter physical appearance, personality characteristics, mannerisms, and life history, so the character who eventually ends up in my story bears little resemblance to his or her real-life counterpart. I may also combine one real-life person with another—

and perhaps even with a third, creating a composite character of all three.

But even if you begin with a real-life role model, avoid an exact life-into-fiction transition. If the person you are writing about is not a public figure, as legally defined, you could face a civil lawsuit, whether justified or not. What to you may be a loving and positive fictional rendition may be to the person in question something else entirely.

With the best of intentions—I wanted to publicly acknowledge her—I once sought to pay tribute to my now deceased mother-in-law in one of my Bart Challis detective novels. For most of her life she had collected spoons (primarily commemorative issues and antiques), which she displayed proudly on wooden racks around her home. When I needed a character with an off-beat occupation for my detective to question, I invented "Tessie Mae Shannon's Spoon Shop." The name was a modified variation of her own. I believed I'd written something she would be proud to show her friends and relatives, but I was wrong. She thought I was making fun of her. And this was a woman who had a superb sense of humor, one of the reasons I thought she would enjoy "her" part in the Challis novel. My intended homage to my mother-in-law fell far short of what I'd envisioned and caused unintended distress in my wife's family.

Friends and relatives can feel hurt and anger at your portrayals of them, even if your intentions are loving and honorable.

Once you've created a realistic fictional character, that person takes on a life you may be unprepared for, doing things or continuing to evolve in ways you hadn't planned.

This is, at least in part, your subconscious at work, adding depth and complexity to what you consciously planned. Sit back and follow your character as you're led into some fresh and surprising scenes and situations.

When Anne Rice began *Interview with the Vampire*, she was writing what she intended to be a short story. Instead, her short story became a long novel as her character took control. The work continued to evolve and eventually became several sequel novels.

When you create fictional characters, use anything from your life, your thoughts, or your emotions that will assist you in building your characters—but take care what you use from *other* people's lives. With forethought and wisdom, the result will likely be characters with depth, people your readers can become personally involved with and will never forget.

# TWENTY TWO 22

## MAKING THE READER CARE:
### DEVELOPING REAL CHARACTERS

When you feel as another feels, that's empathy. In writing, it's achieved when your character is real: three dimensional in all relevant facets and sympathetic enough for your reader to identify with emotionally. No matter what kind of person your character is, readers must be able to recognize aspects of themselves in your fictional creations.

In Stephen King's *The Shining*, the character of young Danny Torrance seeks paternal love; he wants his father, Jack Torrance, to care for him the way his mother does. But during the course of the narrative, his father becomes a lethal madman, and the only thing Danny can do is run from him.

Readers easily identify with this sad, gifted boy. King is a superb storyteller, and a cunning master at character development. Beginning writers would do well to study his novels and note how King builds and maintains depth and believability in his fictional characters.

One evening, over a beer in King's room at a World Fantasy Convention, I asked Steve about the fantastic elements in his work. How did he get away with such outrageous ideas? I remember the smile he gave me.

"First, I break my ass to create absolutely real people," he said. "Once I've done that, once my characters are real, I can take my readers anywhere, into any fantastic situation I conjure up. They'll follow my characters because they *believe* in them."

*The Shining* offers a perfect example of King's writing technique. The Torrance family takes a full hundred pages to reach the Overlook Hotel, and King used these pages to create a completely realistic family—including their background. As a result, once the bizarre events commence at the Overlook, readers accept the fantasy. After all, these things are happening to *real people*. (In Kubrick's film version, Jack was crazy from the outset, which violated King's careful approach.)

Create real people if you want your readers to accept them—and always remember that your protagonist must be *consistent*. You cannot arbitrarily have your character do things which are inconsistent with that person's established personality simply because you want to reach a certain plot point.

As an example, let's say you create a male character who, in childhood, had a near-fatal fall from a barn, from which he developed a severe fear of heights. You cannot then have this character chase the villain over rooftops in a pursuit scene. If the chase *must* take place from a height, then your protagonist should suffer crippling fright during the pursuit, as actor James Stewart did in Hitchcock's film *Vertigo*.

Your protagonist's behavior—and the behavior of all of your characters—should conform to the type of person you have created, and each major character must relate, in a realistic fashion, to the other characters in your story. As Dean Koontz declared, "Fiction is about the interaction of people, about their complex relationships."

The more layers of reality you build into your characters, the more you will cause the reader to care about them. Once readers identify in some way, characters will take on family status in the reader's imagination, and readers will empathize with them.

As a writer, you have an ultimate goal beyond plot and scenes, action and descriptions: Make your characters real.

Make your readers *care*.

# TWENTY THREE 23

## PUTTING YOUR HERO THROUGH THE FIRE:
### BUILDING A FOUNDATION

Max Brand did it best—he put his heroes through bloody hell! By the last page of a typical Max Brand western, the hero had been shot (often several times); he'd been bruised, battered, and wholly exhausted—but he'd survived to defeat the villain and win the woman he loved.

Your protagonist may never be shot to pieces in an Old West epic, but the same principle applies in regard to the trials your character must undergo. Consider, for example, what Ian Fleming did to his character, James Bond, in those 007 thrillers.

"But I don't intend to write adventure novels," you argue.

And I answer that putting your hero through the fire has nothing to do with adventure novels. It's one of the foundations of general literature.

The "fire" your character survives need not be physical—it can be psychological, emotional, or spiritual. Consider Daniel Defoe's *Robinson Crusoe*. But your protagonist *must* battle forces greater than his or her initial self, because this is the means by which your character grows, developing inner strength, endurance, and courage—while demonstrating to his or her own self, as well as to the reader, the ability to prevail over crippling odds.

Your protagonist should have at least one weakness, an Achilles heel, which can be exploited. This is part of the humanity of your character since none of us is perfect. The weakness may be some type of emotional flaw, or it might be a physical handicap. Michael Collins' detective, Dan Fortune, lost an arm.

Your protagonist must be vulnerable to the fires you create to test his or her mettle.

Superman's triumph over his enemies has little personal meaning to most of us, but when a fragile human being, fictional or real, emerges triumphant over severe adversity, we experience relief, and we simultaneously acquire new inner strength. ("If that person got through all this, maybe I could, too!")

For maximum dramatic payoff, subject your protagonist and perhaps several of your main characters to an arduous trial by fire.

Give 'em hell!

## CHARACTER TRANSFORMATION:
### SHOWING HOW CONFLICT AFFECTS YOUR CHARACTERS

One of the signs of a bad novel is that the protagonist emerges at the end of the book unaffected by the events of the narrative. In good novels, and, ideally, in good short stories, the main character is changed by the events of the story. Your protagonist, as first encountered by readers at the outset of the narrative, must emerge altered at the end. You must show not only that he or she has been affected by the emotional or physical conflicts you have created, you must also show this transformation *as it occurs*.

In *Logan's Run*, my protagonist—a Sandman, or police officer of the future—is a stone-cold state assassin who tracks down "runners" who want to live past the age of twenty-one, then terminates them with deadly efficiency. But when he falls in love with Jessica, the sister of a man he previously gunned down, he learns the meaning of life and the rewards it can hold. Thus, Logan is changed: Now he fights to survive, to protect those he has learned to love, and to overcome the system he once embraced.

The same is true of Hemingway's Robert Jordan in *For Whom the Bell Tolls*: Jordan comes to love Maria. By the book's end, he is willing to sacrifice his life for her.

And when Montag, in Bradbury's *Fahrenheit 451*, finally realizes the importance of printed words, he rejects his role as a book burner and joins the book-loving rebels.

As storyteller, your job is to demonstrate human transformation.

Do so, and your fictional characters will achieve maturity, depth, and reality.

## TERMINATING YOUR CHARACTERS:
### DEATH IN FICTION

Y ou have reached the point in your story or novel when it's time for one of your characters to die. Sometimes this is a surprise to you—even a shock, because when you began, you never expected to kill off this particular character. In the course of writing your narrative, you may have become quite fond of this person—wanting him or her to survive—but your plot now dictates that the character must be terminated. Otherwise you won't be true to the natural progression of your story.

There are countless ways to kill off a character in fiction. Here are some examples:

In *The Untamed*, Max Brand created Whistling Dan Barry, an antihero and an expression of the wilderness from which he emerged. He is, by civilized standards, untamed—and he shares a near-mystical kinship with a wild horse called Satan and a fierce wolf-dog, Black Bart.

Brand records their adventures in two sequels, *The Night Horseman* and *The Seventh Man*. At the end of the latter novel Barry has married (which proves to be an uneasy alliance), and he and Kate, his wife, have a daughter named Joan. At the climax of *The Seventh Man* Barry wants to take Joan away, into the wilderness with him, but his wife refuses.

> "You can't have her, Dan....She's my blood,
> my pain, my love, and you want to take her to the

mountains and the loneliness. I'll die to keep her…"
[He moves toward the house.]
"Not a step!" she whispered, and jerked out
her gun. "Not a step!"…
[Dan smiles faintly and starts up the path.]
She had chosen her mark carefully, the upper corner
of the seam of the pocket on his shirt, and before his foot
struck the ground she fired…

He wavered to his knees, and then sank down with his
arms around Black Bart. He seemed, indeed, to crumple
away into the night. …She would have gone to him, but the
snarl of Bart drove her back. Then she saw Satan galloping
up the path and come to a sliding halt where he stood with
his delicate nose close to the face of the master.

There was no struggle with death, only a sigh like the
motion of wind in far off trees, and then, softly, easily, Black
Bart extricated himself from the master, and moved away
down the path, all wolf, all wild. Behind him, Satan whirled
with a snort, and they rushed away into the night, each in an
opposite direction.

The long companionship of the three was ended.

In *Broken Eagle*, Chad Oliver presented his personal version of
the legendary massacre at the Little Bighorn in 1876, when George A.
Custer, with an invading force of 210 men of the Seventh Cavalry, died
on a Montana hillside, slain by Cheyenne and Sioux warriors under
the leadership of Sitting Bull and Crazy Horse.

He smiled, quite relaxed. He saw the sun, swollen and
red. He did not think he would see the sunset.

What did it matter? He had seen so much already. He
had been given so much. Had ever another man had thirty-
six such years? A Boy General, by God! He had been that.
He had stamped his name on history. They all knew him.

George Armstrong Custer!

Libbie, Libbie [Custer's wife], what a love they had
shared. He would not have traded it for anything. He was

where he had chosen to be. ...

He never felt the bullet that slammed into his head.

His last thought as he faced his own sunset was that he had been the luckiest of men.

The classic novel, *A Farewell to Arms*, ends with the death of Catherine, the wartime nurse that Hemingway's protagonist, Frederic Henry, loved so deeply.

> She had one hemorrhage after another. They couldn't stop it. I went into the room and stayed with Catherine until she died. She was unconscious all the time, and it did not take her very long to die. ...I shut the door and turned off the light. It wasn't any good. It was like saying good-bye to a statue. After a while I went out and left the hospital and walked back to the hotel in the rain.

Hemingway later said that he rewrote this ending some twenty-seven times to achieve exactly the correct, stark, objective tone.

In his longest novel, *For Whom the Bell Tolls*, Hemingway's Robert Jordan lies wounded and dying on a rugged mountain slope in Spain. He is tempted to end his life, but convinces himself to wait for a group of enemy troops to come riding into his gun range. Slowing them, killing some of them, will aid the escape of his beloved Maria.

Death is very close to him.

> Think about a cool drink of water...that's what it will be like. Like a cool drink of water. *You're a liar*. It will just be nothing. That's all it will be. Just nothing. Then do it. *Do it*. Do it now. [But] *if you wait and hold them up even a little while, or just get the [lead] officer, that will make all the difference*....He lay very quietly and tried to hold on...[resting] as easily as he could with his elbows in the pine needles and the muzzle of the submachine gun against the trunk of the pine tree... holding onto himself very carefully and delicately to keep his hands steady. He was waiting until the officer reached the sunlit place where the first

trees of the pine forest joined the green slope of the meadow. He could feel his heart beating against the pine needle floor of the forest.

And the novel ends.

The reader knows Jordan will die, but he will not die alone. He will scatter the troops with his gunfire, giving Maria more time to reach safety. (The final shot in the film version has Gary Cooper, as Jordan, firing his submachine gun directly into the camera.)

How have I handled death in my own work? In my science fiction tale, "And Miles To Go Before I Sleep," Murdock, my protagonist, has fallen victim to an alien disease and is dying on a starship far from Earth. As he slips toward oblivion, he thinks about his home planet.

> He remembered his last night on Earth…when he had felt the pressing immensity of the vast universe surrounding him.…He remembered the sleepless hours before dawn when he could feel the tension building within the small white house, within himself, lying there in the heated stillness of the room. He remembered the rain, near morning, drumming the roof and the thunder roaring across the Kansas sky. And then, somehow, the thunder's roar blended into the atomic roar of a rocket, carrying him away from Earth, away to the far stars …away…
> *Away.*
> For Robert Murdock, the journey was over, the long miles had come to an end.
> Now he would sleep forever in space.

There are many moving death scenes recorded in great fiction. If you decide you must kill off one of your characters, create a scene that is vivid and emotionally affecting.

Death is the most intense form of drama, the end of every human road.

Take special care with your death scenes.

Make them memorable.

# IV.

# TECHNIQUES FOR WRITING FICTION

## HOOKING YOUR READER:
### IT TAKES A STRONG LINE TO GET OUT
### OF THE SLUSH PILE

In the early 1960s, when I was managing editor of *Gamma*, a West Coast science fiction/fantasy magazine, I would reserve one morning each week for the slush pile, the stack of unagented stories from new writers who hoped to crack our pages.

I had a sure-fire method of getting through these unsolicited manuscripts. I would pull a story halfway out of its envelope and read the first paragraph. If I liked that paragraph, I'd remove the entire story and read it through. But if the opening paragraph didn't grab me, I'd let the manuscript slide back into its envelope and look for the enclosed return postage. I had just rejected that writer's story.

Brutal, huh? Unfair to those poor writers to judge their entire stories from just the opening paragraph, right?

Wrong.

I was *not* being brutal or unfair. The acid test of any story is its opening. A good story should leap off the page, grab you by the throat, and demand: "Read me!" Something in that first paragraph has to intrigue the reader, whether it is situation, mood, character, or incident.

The "hook" has to be there. Your reader must be involved from the start.

Following are several examples, taken from my own work. Do they hook the reader? You decide.

From "My Name Is Dolly" (*Whispers VI*):

Monday.—Today I met the witch—which is a good

place to start this diary.

I had to look up how to spell it. First I spelled it "dairy," but that's a place you get milk and from *this* you're going to get blood—I hope.

From "The Halloween Man" (*Night Cry*):

Oh, Katie believed in him for sure, the Halloween Man. Him with his long skinny-spindley arms and sharp-toothed mouth and eyes sunk deep in skull sockets like softly glowing embers, charcoal red. Him with his long coat of tatters, smelling of tombstones and grave dirt. All spider-hairy he was, the Halloween Man.

From "The End with No Perhaps" (*Impact 20*):

After he had parked his pink-and-cream Thunderbird at the end of the long gravel drive, Harrison Miller decided that he would like to step on his sunglasses. He got out of the car and removed the hand-tooled leather case his wife, Sylvia, had given him for his birthday; carefully he placed the tinted glasses at his feet. Then he stepped down heavily, grinding the expensive prescription lenses into powder.

From "Jenny Among the Zeebs" (*The Future Is Now*):

What kicked off the hooley was: the zeeb contest had gone sour and *that's* when this zonked-out little chickie wanted to cast some bottoms. It was the two coming together that way, like planets in a collision orbit, that kicked off the hooley.

From "The Final Stone" (*Cutting Edge*):

They were from Indianapolis. Newly married, Dave and *stirring, flexing muscle, feeling power now...anger...a sudden driving thirst for* Alice Williamson, both in their late twenties, both excited about their trip to the West Coast. This would be their last night in Arizona. Tomorrow they planned to be in Palm Springs. To visit Dave's sister. But only one of them would make it to California. Dave, not

Alice. *with the scalpel glittering.*

From "Of Time and Kathy Benedict" (*Whispers V* ):

Now that she was on the lake, with the Michigan shoreline lost to her, and with the steady cat-purr of the outboard soothing her mind, she could think about the last year, examine it thread by thread like a dark tapestry.

From "A Real Nice Guy" (*Mike Shayne's*):

Warm sun.

A summer afternoon.

The sniper emerged from the roof door, walking easily, carrying a custom-leather guncase.

Opened the case.

Assembled the weapon.

Loaded it.

Sighted the street below.

Adjusted the focus.

Waited.

There was no hurry.

No hurry at all.

From "The Day the Gorf Took Over" (*Infinity Two*):

There's a special office at the Pentagon called the Office of Stateside Emergencies. Dave Merkle is in charge, a thin, night-eyed man, haunted by a perpetual sense of failure. He was depressed on the morning of June 3, 1982, because there had not been a decent stateside emergency since early May. There had been three superb overseas emergencies, but they were handled by another office down the hall and didn't count.

From "Into the Lion's Den" (*Alfred Hitchcock*):

Before she could scream, his right hand closed over her mouth. Grinning, he drove a knee into her stomach and stepped quickly back, letting her spill writhing to the floor at his feet. He watched her gasp for breath.

From *The White Cad Cross-Up* (Sherbourne Press):

The Marshal's big automatic crashed twice, and two .45 slugs whacked into my chest. At close range, the force of the bullets drove me back like a boxer's fists, and I landed on the rug, gasping and plenty nervous.

From "Down the Long Night" (*Terror Detective*):

The ocean fog closed in suddenly, like a big gray fist, and Alan Cole stopped remembering. Swearing under his breath, he jabbed the wiper button on the Lincoln's dash, and brought the big car down from fifty to thirty-five. Still dangerous. You couldn't see more than a few yards ahead in this soup. But he said the hell with it and kept the Lincoln at thirty-five because he wanted this mess over in a hurry, because he wanted to hold Jessica in his arms again before the night was done.

From "The Grackel Question" (*Gallery*):

Arnold Hasterbrook I, II, and III was crossing the Greater Continental Federated United States for the sixteen-thousandth time in his customized hoverbug when he saw two lovely hitchies by the side of the road.

From "The Yard" (*Masques II*):

It was near the edge of town, just beyond the abandoned freight tracks. I used to pass it on the way to school in the mirror-bright Missouri mornings and again in the long-shadowed afternoons coming home with my books held tight against my chest, not wanting to look at it.

From "Fair Trade" (*Whispers*):

He tole me to speak all this down into the machine, the Sheriff did, what all I know an' seen about Lon Pritchard an' his brother Lafe an' what they done, one to the other. I already tole it all to the Sheriff but he says for sure that none'a what I tole him happened the way I said it did but to talk it all into the machine anyhow. He figgers to have it all done up on paper from this talkin' machine so's folks kin read it an' laugh at me I reckon.

What do you think? Do these opening paragraphs make the reader sit up and take notice? Are you pulled into the story, your imagination stimulated, your curiosity aroused? Do you want to know *what comes next*? (Editors are *readers*, too, don't forget.)

Sometimes I use a one-line paragraph. A real hook to the gut. Examples:

From "And Miles To Go Before I Sleep" (*Infinity SF* ):
Alone within the great ship, deep in its honeycombed chambers, Robert Murdock waited for death.

From "The Mating of Thirdburt" (*Alien Horizons*):
When Thirdburt turned twenty-one, his father threw him bodily out of the family lifeunit in New Connecticut.

From "Dead Call" (*Frights*):
Len had been dead for a month when the phone rang.

From "The Public Loves a Johnny" (*Impact 20*):
"Lightning!" shouted Ed Fifield, rushing into the kitchen.

From "The Worlds of Monty Wilson" (*Amazing*):
It *looked* like the same world, but it wasn't.

In the pre-comics, pre-television, pre-computer world of writers such as Charles Dickens, readers were comfortable dealing with complex, dense, and longiloquent opening pages in stories and novels. It was an era of leisurely reading, when the pace and style could be deliberate and unhurried, and the reader's attention could be slowly drawn into the narrative.

Not so in today's world.

Today we live in a nano-second-paced, communications-over-loaded, media-dominated society where everything on the planet happens simultaneously and superhumanly fast. Quick, gaudy images flash across our TV screens to grab our attention. Computers and satellite broadcasting take us around the globe in the push of a button. Cell phones are noisily ubiquitous. For a short story or novel to compete, it must waste no time getting off the mark. It must engage the reader's attention *instantly*.

As a writer, you must ask yourself: How can I establish an opening mood that promises danger...thrills...death...exotic adventure? How can I inject the personality of my protagonist into the first paragraph? How can I create a fresh situation that points toward a unique dramatic resolution?

The contemporary writer's challenge is to construct the narrative in a clear, direct manner that says to the reader: Stick with me and I'll frighten you or amaze you...or make you laugh, or cry. I'll take you to places you've never been, and involve you with characters you will find hard to forget.

Right now, go to your bookshelf, or to your local bookstore or public library, and select thirty *recent* novels or stories. Read *only* the first paragraph in each. Then sit down and analyze the elements you discover in each opening. Think about what hooked you, what made *you* want to keep reading. Look for the *Big Four:* situation, mood, character, incident. One or more of these will be present in each of your fifty opening paragraphs.

Take each paragraph apart, word by word. Find out how the writer achieved that particular effect. Then, when it's time for you to begin writing your next story, you will be much better equipped to hook your readers, particularly important if that reader happens to be a magazine or book editor. Hook the editor instantly, and you will have achieved a giant step toward making the sale.

# TWENTY SEVEN 27

## POINT OF VIEW:
### FIRST PERSON? SECOND? THIRD?

As you begin a new project, one of the first decisions you must make is whether to use the first person, second person, or third person viewpoint.

With the first person (*I*), everything in the story is narrated by the protagonist. This is a popular format in hard-boiled detective stories, such as *Red Harvest* by Dashiell Hammett:

> I first heard Personville called Poisonville by a red-haired mucker named Hickey Dewey in the Big Ship in Butte.

When you use the first person perspective, the reader is drawn immediately into the heart of the action and shares each moment of discovery with the narrator. The great strength of this viewpoint is that a powerful sense of intimacy with the reader can be achieved. However, the simultaneous problem is that the reader is able to see and experience only what the narrator sees and experiences. No other point of view is possible.

Second-person (*you*) stories are rare. This form is awkward, and can feel self-conscious and artificial. Readers are usually not comfortable with this format, yet some skilled writers have given us excellent second-person stories. Ray Bradbury's "A Careful Man Dies" offers a prime example:

You sleep only four hours a night. You go to bed at eleven and get up at three. You begin your day then, have your coffee, read for an hour, listen to the faint, far, unreal talk and music of the pre-dawn stations and perhaps you go out for walk. ...so this is how your life goes.

Third-person perspective (*he*, *she*, *it*; also called the *omniscient* viewpoint) is by far the most popular. Although it lacks the immediacy and intimacy of first-person narration, it affords the writer much greater latitude in developing a story or novel, because scenes and characters can be greatly expanded. I used this form for *Logan's Run*, which begins:

Her hair was matted, her face streaked and swollen. One knee oozed slow blood; she'd cut it on a steel abutment. ...She froze, remained motionless. There was someone in the shadows ahead. A silent scream ripped at her throat.

Sandman!

Dean Koontz is a master of the third-person format. In his novels he creates a group of four or five characters and allows the reader to follow each of them in alternating chapters. As each encounters serious danger, he cuts to another character, returning to the first character's hazardous situation in a later chapter. This creates cliff-hanging suspense and moves his cast of characters around his narrative board like pieces in a chess game, with extremely effective results.

A useful exercise for novice writers (and sometimes even for professionals) is to write a section or two of a particular story in each of the three viewpoints. A few paragraphs will be all it takes to gather enough information to decide which format is best suited to that particular work.

This writing exercise is often of great practical assistance to aspiring professional writers because it allows the story itself to reveal to you which form is best.

## DIVING INTO 'THE POOL':
### SHAPING FICTIONAL EFFECTS

As an instructional exercise, I have dissected one of my short stories to demonstrate how I shaped it as I did.

You'll be able to observe how to utilize the opening hook, how to achieve a sense of mounting suspense, and how mood and texture contribute to the story. You'll see how dialogue is employed to move the plot forward and to reveal character, how and when to switch point of view, how the full description of the Creature is delayed, and how sensory description is used to involve the reader.

I will demonstrate precisely how I shaped this story to deliver maximum shock and fright.

I invite you to dive into "The Pool."

The locale is Los Angeles, in the plush area of Bel Air, just beyond Beverly Hills—and I begin with action, with my two main characters in a moving car, making a turn off Sunset Boulevard.

As they turned from Sunset Boulevard and drove past the high iron gates, swan-white and edged in ornamented gold, Lizbeth muttered under her breath.

In this opening sentence, with Lizbeth's reaction to the turn off Sunset, I *immediately* set up tension. She's muttering. Something is wrong.

"What's the matter with you?" Jaimie asked. "You just

said 'shit,' didn't you?

"Yes, I said it."

"Why?"

She turned toward him in the MG's narrow bucket seat, frowning. "I said it because I'm angry. When I'm angry, I say 'shit.'"

"Which is my cue to ask why you're angry."

"I don't like jokes when it comes to something this important."

"So who's joking?"

"You are, driving us here. You said we were going to look at our new house."

"We are. We're on the way."

"This is Bel Air, Jaimie!"

"Right. Says so, right on the gate."

"Obviously, the house isn't in Bel Air."

"Why obviously?"

"Because you made just $20,000 last year on commercials, and you haven't done a new one in three months. Part-time actors who earn $20,000 a year don't buy houses in Bel Air."

"Who says I bought it?"

She stared at him. "You told me you owned it, that it was yours!"

He grinned. "It is, sweetcake. All mine."

"I hate being called 'sweetcake.' It's a sexist term."

"Bullshit! It's a term of endearment."

"You've changed the subject."

"No, you did," he said, wheeling the small sports roadster smoothly over the looping stretch of black asphalt.

Lizbeth gestured toward the mansions flowing past along the narrow, climbing road, castles in sugar-cake pinks and milk-chocolate browns and pastel blues. "So we're going to live in one of these?" Her voice was edged in sarcasm.

Jaimie nodded, smiling at her. "Just wait. You'll see!"

Note that in this exchange between Jaimie and Lizbeth, I use dialogue to characterize them as sharply differing individuals. She's practical, pragmatic, a bit cynical, a romantic at heart. He's easy-going, smotth, a sporty type (drives an MG), willing to gamble with life. (All actors are gamblers.) We learn that he works in commercials but has no guaranteed salary, and that he made only $20,000 the previous year. (This is a very low income by Southern California entertainment-industry standards. The affluent residents of Bel Air normally earn *minimum* annual incomes in the high six figures.)

I also use their exchange to establish a mild conflict between them. Jaimie is a bit of a male chauvinist, and Lizbeth resents this. And she thinks he's lying to her. Already, the reader can begin to relate to them as real people.

Under a cut-velvet driving cap, his tight-curled blond hair framed a deeply tanned, sensual actor's face. Looking at him, at that open, flashing smile, Lizbeth told herself once again that it was all too good to be true. Here she was, an ordinary small-town girl from Illinois, in her first year of theater arts at UCLA, about to hook up with a handsome young television actor who looked like Robert Redford and who now wanted her to live with him in Bel Air!

Lizbeth had been in California for just over a month, had known Jaimie for only half that time, and was already into a major relationship. It was dreamlike. Everything had happened so fast: meeting Jaimie at the disco, his divorce coming through, getting to know his two kids, falling in love after just three dates.

Life in California was like being caught inside one of those silent Chaplin films, where everything is speeded up and people whip dizzily back and forth across the screen. Did she really love Jaimie? Did he really love her? Did it matter?

Just let it happen, kid, she told herself. Just flow with the action.

To set up my narrative viewpoint, I have now entered the mind of

Lizbeth, the true protagonist of the story. I have moved the story from the objective to the subjective. Through her thoughts and memories, we find out why she's here on this particular afternoon with Jaimie—and we learn about her background before they met. (By making her newly arrived in California, the speeded-up aspect of the locale can be explored through her fresh perspective; Jaimie takes it for granted.) We discover why Lizbeth came to California and what she's aiming for as a student. And again, through her, we learn much more about Jaimie: that he is now single, has two children, and is out to score a good time (demonstrated by where they met, in a disco).

We know that Lizbeth is physically attracted to his good looks and smile. (His smile will take on a special significance later in the story.) To Lizbeth, a small-town girl, Southern California offers a life in the fast lane. And she's willing to surrender to this swift, new lifestyle to live with a man she's known for just two weeks. Thus, her life has become dreamlike.

In this section, I have established the locale so that the reader is firmly rooted in the narrative.

"Here we are," said Jaimie, swinging the high-fendered little MG into a circular driveway of crushed white gravel. He braked the car, nodding toward the house. "Our humble abode!"

Lizbeth drew in a breath. Lovely! Perfect!

Not a mansion, which would have been too large and too intimidating, but a just-right two-story Spanish house topping a green-pine bluff, flanked by gardens and neatly trimmed box hedges.

"Well, do you like it?"

She giggled. "Silly question!"

"It's no castle."

"It's perfect! I hate big drafty places." She slid from the MG and stood looking at the house, hands on hips. "Wow. Oh, wow!"

You're right about twenty-thou-a-year actors," he admitted, moving around the car to stand beside her. "This place is way beyond me."

"Then how did you...?"

"I won it at poker last Thursday. High-stakes game. Went into it on borrowed cash. Got lucky, cleaned out the whole table, except for this tall, skinny guy who asks me if he can put up a house against what was in the pot. Said he had the deed on him and would sign it over to me if he lost the final hand."

"And you said yes."

"Damn right I did."

"And he lost?"

"Damn right he did."

She looked at the house and then back at him. "And it's legal?"

"The deed checks out. I own it all, Liz—house, gardens, pool."

"There's a pool?" Her eyes were shining.

He nodded. "And it's a beaut. Custom design. I may rent it out for commercials, pick up a little extra bread."

She hugged him. "Oh, Jaimie! I've always wanted to live in a house with a pool!"

"This one's unique."

"I want to see it."

He grinned and then squeezed her waist. "First the house, then the pool. Okay?"

She gave him a mock bow. "Lead on, master."

In this section, we have arrived at our central arena within the general locale: the house-grounds-pool area, where the real action of the story will be played. But take note: I did not allow Jaimie and Lizbeth to reach this specific area until I had established them fully as realistic characters with whom the reader could comfortably identify.

I now lessen the conflict between them as Jaimie explains to Lizbeth how he came to own the house, admitting that he could never afford it on his own. (I have planted a dramatic seed here, based on both the old saying "nothing in life is free" and the idea that there will be a price to pay for what he won in the game.)

Also—and this is important—I introduce the pool as a subject of conversation *before* I actually allow the reader to see it—thus giving it special dimension and meaning.

> Lizbeth found it difficult to keep her mind on the house as Jaimie led her happily from room to room. Not that the place wasn't charming and comfortable, with its solid Spanish furniture, bright rugs, and beamed ceilings. But the prospect of finally having a pool of her own was so delicious that she couldn't stop thinking about it.
>
> "I had a cleaning service come up here and get everything ready for us," Jaimie proudly told her. He stood in the center of the living room, looking around proudly, reminding her of a captain on the deck of his first ship. "Place needed work. Nobody's lived here in ten years."
>
> "How do you know that?"
>
> "The skinny guy told me. Said he'd closed it down ten years ago, after his wife left him." He shrugged. "Can't say I blame her."
>
> "What do you know about her?"
>
> "Nothing. But the guy's a creep, a skinny creep." He flashed his white smile. "Women prefer attractive guys."
>
> She wrinkled her nose at him. "Like you, right?"
>
> "Right!"
>
> He reached for her, but she dipped away from him, pulling off his cap and draping it over her dark hair.
>
> "You look cute that way," he said.
>
> "Come on, show me the pool. You promised to show me."
>
> "Ah, yes, madame…the pool."

I have now introduced some disquieting elements. Although the house is very attractive, no one has lived in it for a full decade. The reader begins to wonder why the man shut down the place after his wife left. Also, the man is described as "a creep" (i.e., *creepy*). Again, I'm planting seeds in the reader's mind as I move toward my goal of setting up the specific arena of terror—the pool itself. Yet I still do not show the pool to the reader. By keeping Lizbeth away from it, I am teasing the reader, building tension as to what the pool is going to be like. By making Lizbeth anxious to see it, the *reader* becomes anxious—since she is the focal point for reader identification.

They had to descend a steep flight of weathered wooden steps to reach it. The pool was set in its own shelf of woodland terrain, notched into the hillside and screened from the house by a thick stand of trees.

"You never have to change the water," Jaimie said as they walked toward it. "Feeds itself from a stream inside the hill. It's self-renewing. Old water out, new water in. All the cleaning guys had to do was skim the leaves and stuff off the surface." He hesitated as the pool spread itself before them. "Bet you've never seen one like it!"

Lizbeth never had, not even in books or magazine photos.

It was huge, at least ten times larger than she'd expected, edged on all sides by gray, angular rocks. It was designed in an odd, irregular shape that actually made her...made her...suddenly made her...

Dizzy. I'm dizzy.

"What's wrong?"

"I don't know." She pressed a hand against her eyes. "I...I feel a little...sick."

"Are you having your...?"

"No, it's not that. I felt fine until..." She turned away toward the house. "I just don't like it."

"What don't you like?"

"The pool," she said, breathing deeply. "I don't like the pool. There's something wrong about it."

He looked confused. "I thought you'd love it!" His tone held irritation. "Didn't you just tell me you always wanted..."

"Not one like this," she interrupted, overriding his words. "Not this one." She touched his shoulder. "Can we go back to the house now? It's cold here. I'm freezing."

He frowned. "But it's warm, Liz! Must be eighty at least. How can you be cold?"

She was shivering and hugging herself for warmth. "But I am! Can't you feel the chill?"

"All right," he sighed. "Let's go back."

She didn't speak during the climb up to the house.

Below them, wide and black and deep, the pool rippled its dark skin, a stirring, sluggish, patient movement in the windless afternoon.

With this section, I have introduced the pool itself in a very ominous way. Nothing seems normal about it; the pool is so strange ("an odd, irregular shape") that it makes Lizbeth dizzy. She *physically* sensed the evil here, and suddenly has to get away. She is chilled, yet the weather is warm. (I am utilizing the legend that "cold spots" in a house indicate the presence of a ghost.) The fact that only Lizbeth feels the cold tells us that she alone is sensitive to the evil connected with the pool, and the reader strongly sympathizes with her.

Jaimie is set up as the patsy, the fellow who has no sensitivity to the dark things of the world.

And finally, with the last, one-line paragraph, I move the reader a step closer to terror by removing Lizbeth as a screen and allowing the reader to experience the evil directly. Is the pool itself alive? What powers does it possess? What's going to happen to Lizbeth (we *know* it's going to get Jaimie!)?

Upstairs, naked in the Spanish four-poster bed, Lizbeth could not imagine what had come over her at the pool. Perhaps the trip up to the house along the sharply winding road had made her carsick. Whatever the reason, by the time they were back in the house, the dizziness had vanished, and she'd enjoyed the curried chicken dinner Jaimie had cooked for them. They'd sipped white wine by a comforting hearth fire and then made love there tenderly late into the night, with the pulsing flame tinting their bodies in shades of pale gold.

"Jan and David are coming by in the morning," he

had told her. "Hope you don't mind."

"Why should I? I think your kids are great."

"I thought we'd have this first Sunday together, just the two of us, but school starts for them next week, and I promised they could spend the day here."

"I don't mind. Really I don't."

He kissed the tip of her nose. "That's my girl."

"The skinny man…"

"What about him?"

"I don't understand why he didn't try to sell this house in the ten years when he wasn't living here."

"I don't know. Maybe he didn't need the money."

"Then why bet it on a poker game? Surely the pot wasn't anywhere equal to the worth of this place."

"It was just a way for him to stay in the game. He had a straight flush and thought he'd win."

"Was he upset at losing the place?"

Jaimie frowned at that question. "Now that you mention it, he didn't seem to be. He took it very calmly."

"You said that he left after his wife split. Did he talk about her at all?"

"He told me her name."

"Which was?"

"Gail. Her name was Gail."

Having established the aura of evil, I now set up a quiet, romantic interlude, a deliberate change of pace to show how close Lizbeth becomes to Jaimie (making his loss, later in the story, more emotionally painful). Also, I plant the fact that his children will be coming to the house (which will be paid off dramatically at the story's end).

The dialogue is important here: It tells us that the skinny man had no intention of selling the house and only put it up for wager when he thought he had a winning hand. But when he *did* lose it, he made no complaint; what happens to Jaimie is up to fate. He need feel no guilt; the skinny man did not *intend* for Jaimie to die at the house.

And finally, for the first time, we learn the name of the man's wife.

Now, lying in the upstairs bed, Lizbeth wondered what had happened to Gail. It was odd somehow to think that she and the skinny man had made love in this same bed. In a way, she'd taken Gail's place.

Lizbeth still felt guilty about saying no to Jaimie when he'd suggested a postmidnight swim. "Not tonight, darling. I've a slight headache. Too much wine, maybe. You go on without me."

And so he'd gone on down to the pool alone, telling her that such a mild, late-summer night was just too good to waste, that he'd take a few laps around the pool and be back before she finished her cigarette.

Irritated with herself, Lizbeth stubbed out the glowing Pall Mall in the bedside ashtray. Smoking was a filthy habit—ruins your lungs, stains your teeth. And smoking in bed was doubly stupid. You fall asleep…the cigarette catches the bed on fire. She must stop smoking. All it took was some real will power, and if…

Lizbeth sat up abruptly, easing her breath to listen. *Nothing.* No sound.

That was wrong. The open bedroom window overlooked the pool, and she'd been listening, behind her thoughts, to Jaimie splashing about below in the water.

Now she suddenly realized that the pool sounds had ceased, totally.

She smiled at her own nervous reacton. The silence simply meant that Jaimie had finished his swim and was out of the pool and headed back to the house. He'd be there any second.

But he didn't arrive.

This is a transitional section, in which I ease the reader toward oncoming terrors. I have now separated the lovers, isolating my protagonist in the house and situating Jaimie at the pool. I show Lizbeth's apprehensive state of mind, and I use *silence* as an element of suspense. Where is Jaimie, and why hasn't he returned to the bedroom? We *know* that something terrible has happened to him at the pool. But what? Thus, I build my suspense, layer by layer, tighening the story's grip on the reader.

Lizbeth moved to the window. Moonlight spilled across her breasts as she leaned forward to peer out into the night. The pale mirror glimmer of the pool flickered in the darkness below, but the bulk of trees screened it from her vision.

"Jaimie!" Her voice pierced the silence. "Jaimie, are you still down there?"

No reply. Nothing from the pool. She called his name again, without response.

Had something happened while he was swimming? Maybe a sudden stomach cramp or a muscle spasm from the cold water? No, he would have called out for help. She would have heard him.

Then...what? Surely this was no practical joke, an attempt to scare her! No, impossible. That would be cruel, and Jaimie's humor was never cruel. But he might think of it as fun, a kind of hide-and-seek in a new house. *Damn him!*

Angry now, she put on a nightrobe and stepped into her slippers. She hurried downstairs, out the back door, across the damp lawn, to the pool steps.

"Jaimie! If this is a game, I don't like it! Damn it, I mean that!" She peered downward; the moonlit steps were empty. "Answer me!"

Then, muttering "Shit!" under her breath, she started down the clammy wooden steps, holding to the cold iron pipe rail. The descent seemed even more precipitous in the dark, and she forced herself to move slowly.

Reaching level ground, Lizbeth could see the pool. She moved closer for a full view. It was silent and deserted. Where was Jaimie? She suddenly was gripped by the familiar sense of dizzy nausea as she stared at the odd, wierdly angled rock shapes forming the pool's perimeter. She tried to look away. And *couldn't.*

*It wants me!*

That terrible thought seized her mind. But what wanted her? The pool? No...something *in* the pool.

This sequence is the kickoff to the horror that Lizbeth is about to encounter, and the reader is warning her, *don't* go down there, *don't* go to that pool! (Echoes of *Don't open that door!*)

Note the way I have structured this scene and the elements I have used in it. First, Lizbeth is *alone*, and her nakedness makes her vulnerable (as Janet Leigh was vulnerable in *Psycho*.) Putting on the robe does little to lessen her sense of basic vulnerability. The trees screen the pool from her, adding frustration. I use anger as the thing that propels her out of the house, into the hostile dark; she's mad at Jaimie for causing all this.

But at the point I have Lizbeth moving down the steps toward the pool, I switch her mood from anger to wariness, as the descent proves more difficult. Then, as she walks toward the pool, the dizzy nausea returns—and I use the odd *shape* of the pool to help induce it.

Now she's in the orbit of whatever evil is there, in the hypnotic grip of the pool, and it's too late for a retreat. The reader knows Lizbeth can't go back, and with her thought "*it wants me*," the point of ultimate terror has been reached.

The final line reveals, for the first time, that it is not the pool itself that is evil, it's what is *in* the pool. Another layer of suspense has been uncovered—and just as Lizbeth can't look away from the pool, the reader cannot look away from the page.

Note my use of the five senses in this scene: *sound* (as her voice breaks the silence), *touch* ("holding to the cold iron pipe rail"), *sight* (as she sees the pool), *taste* (the nausea), even *smell* in an understated way (one can imagine the odor rising from "the clammy wooden steps").

Thus, I am totally involving the reader in a tactile, fully dimensional environment of dread.

She kicked off the bedroom slippers and found herself walking toward the pool across the moon-sparkled grass, spiky and cold against the soles of her bare feet.

*Stay back! Stay away from it!*

But she couldn't. Something was drawing her toward the black pool, something she could not resist.

At the rocks, facing the water, she unfastened her nightrobe, allowing it to slip free of her body.

She was alabaster under the moon, a subtle curving of leg, of thigh, of neck and breast. Despite the jarring fear hammer of her heart, Lizbeth knew that she had to step forward into the water.

*It wants me!*

The pool was black glass, and she looked down into it, at the reflection of her body, like white fire on the still surface.

Now…a ripple, a stirring, a deep-night movement from below.

Something was coming—a shape, a dark mass, gliding upward toward the surface.

Lizbeth watched, hypnotized, unable to look away, unable to obey the screaming, pleading voice inside her: *Run! Run!*

And then she saw Jaimie's hand. It broke the surface of the pool, reaching out to her.

His face bubbled free of the clinging black water, and acid bile leaped into her throat. She gagged, gasped for air, her eyes wide in sick shock.

It was *part* Jaimie, part something else!

It smiled at her with Jaimie's wide, white-toothed open mouth, but, oh God! only one of its eyes belonged to Jaimie. It had three others, all horribly different. It had *part* of Jaimie's face, *part* of his body.

*Run! Don't go to it! Get away!*

But Lizbeth did not run. Gently, she folded her warm, pinkfleshed hand into the icy wet horror of that hand in the pool and allowed herself to be drawn slowly forward. Downward. As the cold, receiving waters shocked her skin, numbing her, as the black liquid rushed into her open mouth, into her lungs and stomach and body, filling her as a cup is filled, her final image, the last thing she saw before closing her eyes, was Jaimie's wide-lipped, shining smile—an expanding patch of brightness fading down...deep...very deep...into the pool's black depths.

In this section, the horror is fully realized. Lizbeth, under the spell of the thing in the pool, is taken into its depths, drawn there by the hand of her lover. The last image I give the reader is that of Jaimie's smile, a subtle reversal of the norm (death is no smiling matter).

This entire section is deliberately sensual; she is responding, naked and open, to the call of her lover. She gags, is horrified, but finally gives in to the pool-thing. Note that once the water closes over her I do *not* break the sentence; I allow the words and images to carry the reader down with her, all the way to the bottom of the pool.

Jan and David arrived early that Sunday morning, all giggles and shouts, breathing hard from the ride on their bikes.

A whole Sunday with Dad. A fine, warm-sky summer day with school safely off somewhere ahead and not bothering them. A big house to roam in, and yards to run in, and caramel-ripple ice cream waiting (Dad had promised to buy some!), and games to play, and...

"Hey! Look what I found!"

Jan was yelling at David. They had gone around to the back of the house when no one answered the bell, looking for their father. Now eight-year-old Jan was at the bottom of a flight of high wooden steps, yelling up at her brother. David was almost ten and tall for his age.

"What you find?"

"Come and see!"

He scrambled down the steps to join her."

"Jeez!" he said. "A pool! I never saw one this big before!"

"Me neither."

David looked over his shoulder, up at the silent house.

"Dad's probably out somewhere with his new girl-friend."

"Probably," Jan agreed.

"Let's try the pool while we're waiting. What do you say?"

"Yeah, let's!"

They began pulling off their shirts.

My story *could* have ended with Lizbeth's death, but I often enjoy providing what I term a *double climax*, giving the reader another unexpected jolt. When the two kids show up, I change the mood and point of view completely: They arrive in bright sunlight, full of happiness and energy. Then they find the pool, and the reader is shocked to realize they're going to *swim* there. And, like their father, they sense nothing amiss; they are totally unaware of the thing that waits for them.

Motionless in the depths of the pool, at the far end, where rock and tree shadows darkened the surface, it waited, hearing the tinkling high child voices filtering down to it in the sound-muted waters. It was excited because it had never absorbed a child; a child was new and fresh—new pleasures, new strengths.

It had formed itself within the moist deep soil of the hill, and the pool had nurtured and fed it, helping it grow, first with small, squirming water bugs and other yard insects. It had absorbed them, using their eyes and their hard, metallic bodies to shape itself. Then the pool had provided a dead bird, and now it had feathers along part of its back, and the bird's sharp beak formed part of its face. Then a plump gray rat had been drawn into the water, and the rat's glassy became part of the thing's body. A cat had drowned here, and its claws and matted fur added new elements to the thing's expanding mass.

Finally, when it was still young, a golden-haired woman, Gail, had come here alone to swim that long-ago night, and the pool had taken her, given her as a fine new gift to the thing in its depths. And Gail's long silk-gold hair streamed out of the thing's mouth (one of its mouths, for it had several), and it had continued to grow, to shape itself.

Then, last night, this man, Jaimie, had come to it. And his right eye now burned like blue phosphor from the thing's face. Lizbeth had followed, and her slim-fingered hands, with their long, lacquered nails, now pulsed in wormlike convulsive motion along the lower body of the pool-thing.

Now it was excited again, trembling, ready for new bulk, new lifestuffs to shape and use. It rippled in dark anticipation, gathering itself, feeling the pleasure and the hunger.

Faintly, above it, the boy's cry: "Last one in's a fuzzy green monkey!"

It rippled to the vibrational splash of two young bodies striking the water.

It glided forward swiftly toward the children.

Thus, I end the story from the viewpoint of the horror within the pool. Only at this very late point do I allow the reader to know just what is down there, how it was formed, and what it actually looks like. Many beginning writers make the mistake of telling too much too soon, at the start of their story. I create an element of mystery with the thing in the pool; I withhold its shape and function until the final page.

I always take great care with the closing line. Ideally, the line should leave the reader with yet more terrors to be realized beyond the end of the narrative itself—my *echo effect*.

What I have done with "The Pool," in the way of detailed analysis, *you* can do with stories of your own choosing. Select a story that you liked the first time you read it. Carefully reread it. Get the overall story fixed in your mind. Then go back and read it section by section, breaking it down as to basic structure, plot elements, characterization, and conflict. Dissect it; find out why the story is successful, and exactly *how* the author achieved suspense. Note how narrative, viewpoint, and dialogue illuminate situations and locales, how actions are related to character, and how the author builds to the climax.

This kind of analysis will help you understand the mechanics of fiction. You can do the same thing, on a larger scale, with favorite novels. The process is similar to taking apart the engine of a car to see how the parts all work together to produce the power. Once you understand how it's been done by other writers, you can successfully build your own fictional engines.

Analysis pays.

# TWENTY NINE 29

## EMPLOYING THE FIVE SENSES: GIVE YOUR STORIES DEPTH

We human beings have five physical senses: touch, hearing, smell, sight, taste.

The best writing employs all five of these basic senses because sensory impressions create depth in stories and novels. It is not necessary to use all five in the same scene, but the writer should always be aware of where each sensory insertion is best placed.

Touch: The barrel of the automatic was cold and smooth against the skin of his hand.

Hearing: Her shocked scream drew him quickly toward the slumbering house.

Smell: The room reeked of burned cordite and metal-dusted blood.

Sight: Her hair flowed rhythmically, dancing gold and amber against the sunlit window.

Taste: He sipped cautiously at the cracked mug and tasted the coffee, strong and black and bitter.

When all of the senses are employed in a story, the reader becomes completely involved. Apparent reality is heightened, allowing a deeper level of communication to be achieved between writer and reader. Three-dimensional characters perceive their reality and their worlds through all five physical senses. Use all of them, as appropriate, to skillfully achieve your creative goals.

# THIRTY 30

## DESCRIBING YOUR FICTIONAL WORLDS:
### WHILE KEEPING YOUR PLOT IN FOCUS

Several years ago I was browsing through various tomes at a Los Angeles bookstore. I picked up a collection of modern British short stories, read the opening page of the lead story, and was stunned. The author had her protagonist open the door to a London flat. She then described every item in that room in careful detail: the pattern of wood on the door, the color and texture of the rug, every table and chair, the curtains over the windows, and the dust motes floating in the air!

I shook my head in disbelief. I found no plot point that related to this excessive wordage, no dramatic reason for it other than the author's compulsion to describe every item that could possibly fit into a London flat.

Perhaps this sort of thing is common in U.K. literature. I don't read much British short fiction, so I can't speak with authority. But as a writer who has always sought economy in prose, I was appalled at this rampant use of verbiage.

How much is too much?

This is for you—the creator—to decide. However, what you describe should be relevant to your plot, characterization, and action. For example, since readers are presumably familiar with the interior of typical motel rooms, it is seldom necessary to describe their contents in detail. But if some particular object, color, or sensation stands out in the eyes or nose of your protagonist, then you need to describe it because it is relevant.

My personal style is to keep description to a minimum. In my story, "A Good Day," when the protagonist reaches his mother's house, I use only a few bare words of description to set my scene:

> Ma's place was good to see again. Just a plain weathered house with a black tar roof stuck in beside some big oaks with plowed ground behind and a rusty Dodge truck in the driveway.

I never describe more than is necessary. I don't want to bore my readers with excess description if a few, well-chosen words will do the job.

Sometimes, depending on the story line, an extended description is in order. If an object is important to the plot, then it should be described in proportion to its importance.

When Ray Bradbury's dinosaur hunters, in "A Sound of Thunder," finally encounter a fearsome tyrannosaurus rex, the massive beast is described in careful detail as the center of action:

> It came on great oiled, resilient, striding legs. It towered thirty feet above the trees, a great evil god, folding its delicate watchmaker's claws close to its oily reptilian chest. Each lower leg was a piston, a thousand pounds of white bone, sunk in thick ropes of muscle, sheathed over in a gleam of pebbled skin like the mail of a terrible warrior. Each thigh was a ton of meat, ivory, and steel mesh. And from the great breathing cage of the upper body, those two delicate arms dangled out front, arms with hands that might pick up and examine men like toys, while the snake neck coiled. And the head itself, a ton of sculptured stone, lifted easily upon the sky. Its mouth gaped, exposing a fence of teeth like daggers. Its eyes rolled, ostrich eggs, empty of all expression save hunger. It closed its mouth in a death grin. It ran, its pelvic bones crushing aside trees and bushes, its taloned feet clawing damp earth, leaving prints six inches deep wherever it settled its weight. It ran with a gliding ballet step, far

too poised and balanced for its ten tons. It moved into a sunlit arena warily, its beautifully reptile hands feeling the air.

A lengthy description is justified here because the T-rex is the true focus of Bradbury's story. Every word he uses counts in creating this awesome creature.

Description is one of the most important tools a writer uses to create a fictional world for readers, who see only what you allow them to see, and only in the order in which you present your images.

When Philip Marlowe, Raymond Chandler's detective (in the magazine version of "The Lady in the Lake"), enters the house of a man named Godwin, Chandler's description slowly reveals what is found there:

> [He] was sitting in a deep brocade chair with his slippered feet on a footstool that matched the chair. He wore an open-neck polo shirt and ice cream pants and a white belt. His left hand rested easily on the wide arm of the chair and his right hand drooped languidly outside the other arm to the carpet, which was a solid dull rose. He was a lean, dark, handsome guy, rangily built. One of those lads who move fast and are much stronger than they look. His mouth was slightly open showing the edges of his teeth. His head was a little sideways, as though he had dozed off as he sat there, having himself a few drinks and listening to the radio.
>
> There was a gun on the floor beside his right hand and there was a scorched red hole in the middle of his forehead.

Only with Chandler's last line of description do we learn that the man has been shot to death. Everything Chandler describes leads to the payoff of this final line.

Description may be used in many ways, but the danger for the novice writer lies in the tendency to over-describe. Confine your description to what your reader *needs* to perceive—what is necessary to advance your narrative.

Nothing more.

Anything else, for the beginning writer, is excessive.

# THIRTY ONE 31

## DIALOGUE:
### WHAT IT IS—AND WHAT IT ISN'T

Dialogue in a short story or novel is never realistic. If fictional dialogue were printed as it is actually spoken in real life, readers would quickly become frustrated and bored, because real-life dialogue is verbose, repetitive, usually rambles, and is often shallow.

When writing scripts for TV or films, spoken words must be stripped to the bone. Most actors and directors hate long speeches. (When presented with a new script, the first thing actor Steve McQueen did was to delete half of his character's dialogue. Anything he could get across to the audience with facial expression or body language—rather than speech—was excised from the written script words he was supposed to say.)

In prose, dialogue can be extended to greater length than in scripts; it need not be as terse or pointed. But never, neither in prose nor in script, is dialogue ever true to life.

The key to effective fictional dialogue is that it must *appear* to be realistic, however. Readers must be able to believe that characters actually talk this way. Beneath the surface, though, dialogue must carry subtext designed to advance the narrative, to illumine character, to reveal emotional truths, to set the mood, and to clarify plot points.

One effective way to perceive dialogue is to think of it as *action*.

Ernest Hemingway, considered to be a master of dialogue, was never realistic in its presentation as clearly demonstrated in "The Killers," his classic short story.

"We're going to kill a Swede. Do you know a big Swede named Ole Andreson?"

"Yes."

"He comes here to eat every night, doesn't he?"

"Sometimes he comes here."

"He comes here at six o'clock, don't he?"

"What are you going to kill Ole Andreson for? What did he ever do to you?"

"He never had a chance to do anything to us. He never even seen us."

"And he's only going to see us once," Al said.

F. Scott Fitzgerald was more formal in his use of dialogue. He allowed his characters to express themselves in a relaxed, but also controlled, manner. Here's an exchange from "Three Hours Between Planes":

"Have a highball?" she asked. "No? Please don't think I've become a secret drinker, but this was a blue night. I expected my husband and he wired he'd be two days longer. He's very nice, Donald, and very attractive. Rather your type and coloring." She hesitated, "and I think he's interested in someone in New York—and I don't know."

"After seeing you it sounds impossible," he assured her. "I was married for six years and there was a time I tortured myself that way. Then one day I just put jealousy out of my life forever. After my wife died I was very glad of that. It left a very rich memory—nothing marred or spoiled or hard to think over."

Raymond Chandler often used dialogue to deliver wisecracks in his meticulously styled detective novels. He employed hard language to impart his own cynical view of the contemporary society he was a part of, as the following dialogue from *The Big Sleep* proves:

"So you're tough tonight," Eddie Mars' voice said [over the phone].

"Big, fast, tough, and full of prickles. What can I do for you?"

"Cops over there—you know where. You keep me out of it."

"Why should I?"

"I'm nice to be nice to, soldier. I'm not nice not to be nice to."

"Listen hard and you'll hear my teeth chattering."

In his early work in the 1940s, Ray Bradbury often used dialogue to set up the tension of his story. As in his opening for "The Wind":

The phone rang at six-thirty that evening. It was December and already dark as Thompson picked up the phone.

"Hello."

"Hello, Herb?"

"Oh, it's you, Allin."

"Is your wife home, Herb?"

"Sure. Why?"

"Damn it."

Herb Thompson held the receiver quietly. "What's up? You sound funny."

"I wanted you to come over tonight."

"We're having company."

"I wish you could come over tonight."

"Wish I could. Company and all. My wife'd kill me."

"I wish you could come over."

"What's it—the wind again?"

"Oh, no. No."

"Is it the wind?" asked Thompson.

The voice on the phone hesitated. "Yeah. Yeah, it's the wind."

In my own work I'm always aware of what dialogue must accomplish. I often allow my characters to tell each other things the reader needs to know. As in my story "The Halloween Man":

Katie asked him if he'd ever seen a demon.

"Sure, I seen one," said Todd Pepper. "The old Halloween Man, I seen him. Wears a big pissy-smelling hat and carries a bag over one shoulder, like Santa. But he's got no toys in it, nosir. Not in *that* bag!"

"What's he got in it?"

"Souls. That's what he collects. Human souls."

Katie swallowed. "Where where does he get them from?"

"From kids. Little kids. On Halloween night."

Norman Mailer, in *The Naked and the Dead*, made dialogue serve his bitter view of war:

"Take it easy," a soldier said from a nearby cot.

Minneta threw his magazine at him, and screamed, "There's a Jap outside the fuggin tent, there's a Jap right over there, right over there." He looked about wildly, and shouted, "Where's a gun, gimme a gun."

Dialogue is one of the fundamental elements of fiction. Study how the prose masters employ dialogue in their work, and the impact of your own work will be substantially amplified.

# THIRTY TWO 32

## *SUSPENSE:*
### *HOW TO ACHIEVE IT*

Dashiell Hammett once declared that "suspense is when nothing happens." He meant that what the reader thinks *might* happen is far more suspenseful than what *is* happening.

Suspense is often achieved by anticipation.

Hammett's classic novel, *The Maltese Falcon*, constantly promises violence and bloodshed, yet in reality, it is no more than a series of carefully staged dialogues. Each scene builds toward violence and gunplay, yet the murders occur off-scene. Hammett achieves exceptional tension and suspense by what he *suggests* will happen. The reader is kept constantly on edge until a double climax is reached: first, when the statue of the fabled black bird turns out to be worthless, and second, when Sam Spade makes the decision to turn over to the police the person who killed his partner, a murderer who is also the woman he loves.

By contrast, in overt action, there is no build-up of suspense. Excitement, yes. Vicarious thrills, certainly. But not true suspense.

Suspense is achieved when a strong sense of anticipation is created. Who is going to die next? Will the hero survive? How will the protagonist's problems be solved? Will he or she escape the trap? All are matters of suspense.

Keep your readers guessing. Keep them off-balance. Keep surprising them with new twists and turns. Keep them anticipating.

Keep them in suspense.

# THIRTY THREE 33

## STAY WITH THE HEAT:
### DON'T STOP UNTIL THE END

One of the most important rules of writing is: *Finish what you begin!*

I have heard beginning writers complain: "But when I get half-way through, I see how much revision is needed. That's why I go back and start over."

No! No! No!

When you're rolling with a story, do *not* stop to revise. Let your heat and creative passion carry you through to the end. Then and only then should you go back and revise. You will always have plenty of time to revise after you've completed a full first draft.

*Logan's Run* is a good example. When I was writing the novel with George Clayton Johnson, and we were about a third of the way into our first draft, George declared that we should stop so we could revise the early chapters.

"Not on your life!" I told him. "We need to get the whole story down on paper, before we start to revise. If we stop now, we'll lose our momentum. We keep going, George. We run with Logan."

And we did, spelling each other at the typewriter in a Malibu motel room, finishing that first draft in just three weeks of heated writing. We ran with Logan, allowing him to lead us from one adventure to the next. This is true with many stories and novels. The character seems to take over while you, the writer, are suddenly following your creation as you record that character's actions—a most mystical process!

Once we had finished a full draft of the Logan novel, I took it away from George and went north to San Francisco, where I revised, tightened, and polished the manuscript.

Back in Los Angeles, George okayed what I'd done, added a bit here and there, and that was it. We had our novel.

If we'd stopped at the one-third point to revise, *Logan's Run* may never have been finished.

Stay with the heat.

Finish what you begin!

# Thirty Four 34

## DEVELOPING CONFLICT:
### SHOW YOUR CHARACTER PREVAILING

In every story or novel the protagonist begins with a goal: to find love, defeat an enemy, overcome an illness, uncover a treasure, win a battle, achieve success, escape impending danger, or (as with Logan, my protagonist in *Logan's Run*), simply to survive.

The goal of your protagonist provides you, as writer, with the basis for conflict. To win, your protagonist must surmount the barriers that prevent the goal from being realized. And there must be a "dark hour" when the task seems hopeless.

*The Writer's Journey: Mythic Structure for Writers*, by Christopher Vogler, discusses this process clearly and in detail. *The Writer's Journey* is an essential book in any fiction or scriptwriter's library, most particularly if you have any aspirations to sell film rights to your work in the future. As a beginning writer, this should be the next book you read or buy.

Every story requires some element of emotional or physical conflict (or a combination of both). From the standpoint of writing structure, your character's goal can *only* be attained through struggle and adversity.

American readers want your character to prevail. They want your hero to reach his or her goal, and they will generally be dissatisfied if, in the end, the hero fails. This is not necessarily true for European or Asian readers. Even in stories geared to American audiences, however, sometimes your protagonist will fail—not all American-written stories have happy endings—but in these cases, the battle between the story's protagonist and antagonist must be fairly waged.

Conflict ("the battle") is an essential element in all fiction. Without it, you have no fictional story to tell.

Create the goal, develop the story's internal conflict, have your protagonist surmount the challenges caused by conflict, and then—as your character prevails—so will your reader.

It is this vicarious success that will keep your readers coming back to you for more.

# Thirty Five 35

## CLIMAX AS RESOLUTION:
### MOVING THE STORY TO CLOSURE

Each scene in a successful story moves the narrative toward its climax (the major turning point)—often the point of highest dramatic tension. This forward progression may be subtly accomplished, scene to scene, but the generally upward movement must never cease. Forward momentum must always occur, even in scenes that, on the surface, appear tranquil.

The climax of a story or novel is the physical and/or emotional payoff, the time when the protagonist's goal has either been realized or aborted, and the plot problem has been resolved. For the reader, it is the time when closure is achieved.

And because climax is the resolution of a story's conflict, once the climax has been reached, the story is over. If loose ends regarding plot or characters remain to be explained, this must be accomplished swiftly—without excess verbiage—so your story may be decisively concluded to the reader's satisfaction.

# THIRTY SIX 36

## THE RIGHT ENDING:
### A CLEAR AND GRATIFYING CONCLUSION

The ending to your story must satisfy the reader. It must be emotionally gratifying and a logical culmination of your plot, the apparently inevitable result of the events you set in motion earlier in your narrative.

Readers must be prepared for your ending. Although they love to be surprised, they don't want to be confused. All surprises in story endings must be consistent with your plot and characters, as well as the rules of common sense and logic. Never leave your reader wondering: "What was *that* all about?" Endings must be clear and reasonable.

And they should not appear to be forced. They must grow naturally from the soil of your narrative—from the plot, the characters, and the challenges that have confronted your characters.

My story "The Cure" is about an emotionally tortured strangler who is compulsively driven to kill. He wants to end this deadly pattern, but doesn't know how. In the ending, he encounters McGrath, an ex-surgeon, who offers a "cure." My ending:

> The cure is almost complete He took the last one yesterday and it's fine. He's an expert and I don't have any worries. I'll never kill again, just like McGrath promised, no matter if I get the compulsion or not, because you can't strangle anybody without fingers and thumbs.
>
> And I don't have any more of those.

In my story "Dead Call," the narrator is talked into suicide by Len (a deceased friend), who uses a telephone as his means of ghostly communication. The narrator is now poised to talk others into the act of self-destruction. I end my story by having him address the reader directly:

> I've been dead for a month now, and Len was right. It's fine here. No pressures. No worries. Gray and quiet and beautiful...
>
> I know how lousy things have been for you. And they're *not* going to improve.
>
> Isn't that your phone ringing?
>
> Better answer it.
>
> It's important that we talk.

In "Encounter with a King," Dancer Webb, a young boxer on his way up, is slated to fight an over-the-hill veteran who is, as the story opens, but a shadow of the competitor he once was. Win or lose, it's the veteran's last fight. The young boxer finds that he cannot bring himself to destroy this gallant man and allows the veteran to win. Dancer's manager, Spec Leonard, believes that only destroyers survive to become champions. Deciding that his young boxer has gone soft, he walks out on Dancer after the fight. I end with:

> A crack had opened, a fault in his career that had been there all along, and it could never be closed.
>
> "Listen, kid, don't you worry," Patchey was telling him. "Spec'll be back. Hell, he never walked out on a fighter yet. You watch, he'll be back."
>
> "Sure," said Dancer softly, his eyes still closed, feeling the pain again, "he'll be back."

The reader knows that Spec will never be back, and that Dancer's once promising career is now over Thus, my ending directly results from the narrative's prior events.

Writers often employ irony to end stories. In "A Real Nice Guy" I dramatize a scene between two strangers. Jimmie (who the reader knows to be a vicious, cold-blooded sniper) goes to bed with Janet. At the end, she shoots him from a rooftop as he exits an apartment building. Turns out they were *both* snipers, though neither knew the truth about the other, and irony is thereby achieved in my closing paragraphs:

> Poor Jimmie, she thought. It was just his bad luck to meet me. But that's the way it goes.
>
> Janet Lakely had a rule, and she never broke it: When you bed down a guy in a new town, you always target him the next day. She sighed. Usually it didn't bother her. Most of them were bastards. But not Jimmie. She'd enjoyed talking to him, playing her word games with him…bedding him. She was sorry he had to go.
>
> He seemed like a real nice guy.

The tone of your ending can vary, culminating in either joy or despair. However, in professional writing you are given the freedom to employ negative, unhappy endings in short stories much more frequently than is possible in commercial novels. In the longer form, readers have sweated out the dangers and the trials with your protagonist, and they want to share his or her final victory. Otherwise, they feel cheated. They've invested considerable time and emotion in reading your novel—most novels these days are over three hundred pages—and it's a disappointment to them if things turn out badly.

Sometimes a happy ending leaves the characters with a job to yet be done before ultimate happiness can be realized. In Dean Koontz's ending to *Midnight*, he effectively demonstrates how this sort of ending is constructed:

> Scott had stopped struggling. He was probably just exhausted. Sam was sure that he had not really gotten through the boy's rage. Hadn't more than scratched the surface…They had a long way to go, months of struggle, maybe even years…The battle for Scott had only begun.
>
> But it *had* begun. That was the wonderful thing. It *had* begun.

Other happy endings can involve a change of locale for the surviving characters. They want to get away, to escape, to find a fresh environment in which to begin their new lives.

Peter Straub offers us an example of this approach on the final page of *If You Could See Me Now*:

> She straightened her back on the seat beside me. There [was] no more crying…"Let's just drive," she said. "I don't want to see Zack…we can write from wherever we get to."
> "Fine," I said.
> "Let's go to someplace like Wyoming or Colorado."
> "Whatever you want," I said.

Many writers like to wait until the last line to deliver their final shock. From "Two Bottles of Relish," Lord Dunsany's story of cannibalism:

> They walked through our sitting room in silence… and together they went into the hall, and there I heard the only words they said to each other. It was the inspector who first broke that silence.
> "But why," he said, "did he cut down the trees?"
> "Solely," said Linley, "in order to get an appetite."

Another fine example of a final shock is from Bradbury's graveyard gem, "The Emissary":

> Dog was a bad dog, digging where he shouldn't. Dog was a good dog, always making friends. Dog loved people. Dog brought them home.
> And now, moving up the dark hall stairs, at intervals, came the sound of feet, one foot dragged after the other, painfully, slowly, slowly, slowly.
> Dog shivered. A rain of strange night earth fell seething on the bed.
> Dog turned.
> The bedroom door whispered in.

Martin had company.

Endings can be happy or unhappy, ironic or shocking, light or dark, but whatever ending you choose, it must *fit*.

I'm going to conclude this section with a full printing of my story, "Just Like Wild Bob." It is about a strained father-son relationship, and how a single end comment from the father affects the young protagonist. Note that my ending is the natural result of the story's previous action.

## Just Like Wild Bob

It was hot, desperately hot in the Ford, and McAllister felt the heat under his clothes, felt the perspiration gathering beneath his armpits and along his trousered thighs. Damn the California sun, he thought, and damn having to drive through it in an old heap of a '51 Ford with 90,000 wearing miles on the odometer.

He looked over at his father, who sat bolt upright in the heat, as straight as a soldier. And Paul McAllister thought: nothing bothers him, he just sits there in this blast-furnace air and nothing bothers him at all. My God, I hope things like heat and cold and long rides bother me when I'm eighty; I hope to God they do. He isn't even human. He's some kind of insensitive machine that keeps on operating no matter what happens to it. People look at him and say: isn't he wonderful, isn't it *grand* to be that way? And I feel like yelling at them, McAllister thought. I feel like yelling: you think he's so damn wonderful and grand why don't you take him to live with you? Why don't *you* put up with his senility and his deafness and his dirt? You'd soon find out how grand he is.

Highway 99 ribboned ahead of them, flat and gray-white, rippling slightly in the heat-haze. Paul held the Ford at sixty-five. Not fast on a week day like this with no cops out, but plenty fast for the old Ford. It rolled and heaved drunkenly around curves and on a straight like this it took both hands to keep it steady at anything over fifty.

The thing is, I should have gone to San Berdoo without him, McAllister told himself; I should have said: hell no you can't go with me! This is business and I have to see this guy about something you wouldn't understand... But his father had begged to be taken along, whined like a puppy, and McAllister had given in. Hours up and hours back in the August heat with the sun strong enough to suck the water from a camel's hump—but the old man had not complained once. He knew better. If he said a word McAllister would cut him to pieces with his tongue. He'd done it often enough before.

I'm thirty-one and he's eighty and he's got no business messing up my life, McAllister's inner monologue continued. I ought to be married, have a wife and family of my own—and maybe I would if it weren't for him. Oh, well, I guess I wouldn't, but hell, who knows, really, whether I would or not? He's always there, around the house all day like some kind of vulture, crouched over the TV, maybe an inch from the screen because of his eyes, always giving me terrible suggestions about how to sell real estate, about what to say to people.

If Mother were alive things might be different. They *would* be, no doubt of it. She'd let him talk to her while she ironed or cooked and the words would go on past her because she never really listened to him, never really heard the same tired, dreadful stories over and over. The words would disappear in her mind like invisible ink on white paper.

But with her gone, he's just got me. Only me. And I can't ignore him the way Mother could. When I'm home he's talking all the time and I keep wanting to tell him to shut up, to shut his damn old mouth up, that I've heard all he's got to say a million times and just can't stand the words any longer. And sometimes, McAllister told himself with a bitter satisfaction, sometimes I *do* just that. I yell like fury at him and he shuts up for maybe an afternoon—or even an entire day—and pouts like a slapped kid.

The old man coughed violently next to McAllister. He pulled a gray handkerchief from his pants pocket and began to dab his watering eyes with it.

"My God, *look* at that thing!" snapped McAllister. "I told you to make sure you had a clean one before you left."

"Sorry," the old man said, and smiled toothlessly. "Sorry, son, but I forgot to get another one from the drawer. I did."

"All right," Paul sighed. "But just put it away. You'll fill the car with germs."

McAllister's father nodded in the heat, his long yellow-white hair pasted thinly to his lined forehead. He looked over at his son and attempted another smile, but to Paul it was a grimace, a toothless grimace—and perversely, Paul did not smile back.

"You didn't *have* to go along, you know," he told his father, eyes coldly fastened on the road ahead. "I warned you about the heat."

The old man seemed puzzled. "I didn't say nothing about the heat, did I?" he asked. "I didn't say nothing."

McAllister sighed again and kept his eyes on the wide, flat highway running up into the hills. Sweat had gathered like a cluster of tiny seed-pearls on his upper lip and he ran the edge of his left sleeve over the skin, immediately angry with himself for not using his clean handkerchief and showing his father what it meant to carry fresh, laundered things.

Hell, he'd live like a pig if I ever left him, McAllister assured himself. He never washes really well, just kind of *pats* some water over him when he's in the tub. His bath towel shows it. Why is it that old people are so dirty? Not all of them, though. My grandfather on my mother's side was as neat as a pin right up to the day he died. And he was eighty-three. Yet most old people would live like pigs if they could.

A half-mile ahead of them, near the right side of the highway, McAllister made out a small figure, waving. As they drew nearer he braked to forty-five and squinted for a clearer look. A boy of maybe eighteen in blue denims with sandy, crew cut hair was waving and shouting something. Just a few feet behind the boy, completely off the highway on the grass verge, McAllister saw a light-green panel truck. Gas, that's it, thought Paul; the kid's out of gas.

"There's a guy stuck up ahead," McAllister told his father. "I'm going to stop and give him a lift."

"Fine with me," the old man replied. "That's all right."

Paul had never believed in picking up hitchhikers. Never can tell about them. Maybe only one in a thousand's a sour apple, but he might be the one you pick up. Might be he's got a gun and he needs your car for some kind of getaway. But not this kid, McAllister was certain, not this kid here in the middle of the open highway in broad daylight with his own panel truck. Not a chance in a million. I'd be a heel if I passed him by.

McAllister brought the Ford to a halt by the truck and motioned to the boy in the denims. "Need a ride?" he asked.

"Sure do, mister," answered the boy, trotting over to the car. "Ran plain out of gas about a mile back and just coasted this far hoping I'd make a station. But don't seem like there's one around for miles."

"That's right," said Paul. "Nearest station is a good bit up the highway. Hop in. I'll take you. It's on the way."

"Thanks a lot," the boy said and was about to open the front door when Paul said: "Get in back. More room there."

"Okay." The boy slid into the rear of the Ford, slamming the door. McAllister accelerated away, leaving the green panel truck parked and silent behind them in the heat.

"My name is Springer," the boy said from the back seat. "Anson Springer."

"Mine's Paul McAllister," said Paul mechanically, watching the road. "This is my father."

"Hi," said the boy.

"Glad to make your acquaintance," smiled the old man, twisting in the seat and extending one withered yellow hand. The boy shook it briskly. "Same here."

"You work around these parts?" the old man asked—and Paul thought: hell, he's got someone to listen to him now and he's going to start talking up a storm. Maybe picking up this kid was a lousy idea after all. Dad knows when I'm sore and he stays quiet, but give him an extra pair of ears to bend and off he goes.

"I'm a mechanic in L.A.," replied the boy. "I help my brother in his garage."

"Then…you know cars, eh boy?" The old man twisted even farther around in the seat.

"Yeah, a little I guess." He hesitated. "I can take an engine apart if that's what you mean."

"Ever hear about a car called the Stevens-Duryea?" The old man's voice held a trace of urgency, of tenseness, and McAllister drew in a sharp breath and swore silently. God, he's going to start the business about the early days; he's going to go into the whole long, involved, exhausting bit.

"I doubt if he's ever heard of the car, Dad," said Paul, forcing a degree of pleasantness into his voice. He flicked his glance to the rearview mirror, hoping the boy would back up his statement. If so, the talk could be slanted, pushed away from the familiar subject at hand.

"As a matter of plain fact," the boy grinned, "I sure have. I mean, I've seen pictures of it. My brother's an old-car bug. Knows all about Barney Oldfield and like that."

From the corner of his eye McAllister could see his father straighten in triumph and nod quickly like a bird, the wrinkles on his veined neck folding deeply one upon another. It was too late now. When the boy mentioned Barney Oldfield McAllister realized it was too late.

"I knew him," piped the old man, still nodding. "Yes, sir, I knew Barney. I raced against him when he drive a White Steamer in Missouri. Big White Steamer down in Missouri. Cross-country it was, maybe 200 miles, through mud so deep you could swim in it. I was in a Chalmers-Bluebird then and I let Barney break ground for me. I mean following his big Steamer, staying right in his tracks while all the other cars bogged down. Near the end of the race old Barney he ran out of water and had to stop and leave his car on the road while he went to a farmhouse and asked for some. For the Steamer, you know. Had to have water for the Steamer."

Paul made one more desperate attempt. "Maybe he doesn't want to hear all about that stuff, Dad," McAllister said, his voice now edged and crisp. "It's a pretty damn hot day and maybe—"

"Oh no, I'm glad to listen," the boy cut in. "Golly!... Al—that's my brother, Al—he'll be mighty surprised when I tell him I met somebody that actually raced Barney Oldfield. Did you finally beat him, Mr. McAllister?"

Paul sighed and kept his eyes fixed on the road. It was no use, none at all, and now all he could hope for was a gas station. He pressed his foot down on the pedal and the speedometer needled up to sixty-eight, then seventy. The Ford began to shudder and Paul eased off. No use wrecking the car just to keep from hearing it all again, he thought. Won't be much longer. We'll get there soon. I know there's a new station opened up about five miles or so down the highway.

"Well, I never *did* beat ole Barney," his father was saying. "I passed him when he went for water that time, but my car threw a rod and I never finished that race at all. Ole Barney, he won fair an' square."

I doubt if Oldfield ever drove a White Steamer, McAllister thought bitterly. Sure, you probably raced a couple of times, but I bet you never came any closer to Oldfield than a sparrow comes to a hawk.

"I knew Bobby Burman, too," the old man went on, warming to his subject. His eyes began to water under the wrinkled lids and he blinked rapidly. "We called him Wild Bob because he was a regular hellion behind the wheel. This was 1909 you know, and he used to come out to Missouri and race at the Elm Ridge track." The old man took out his gray handkerchief and scrubbed at his watering eyes.

Filthy, thought McAllister; that's just plain filthy. You can't tell an old man anything. Tell him to keep that thing out of sight and he'll be blowing his nose with it in front of the Queen of England five minutes later! Like a three-year-old. You can't tell them anything they remember.

"Wild Bob was in a Stoddard-Dayton out at Elm Ridge one Sunday," the old man continued, "and it was beginning to rain cats and dogs. Well, Bobby was cuttin' up the track, you know, with that big car of his, and so I went out to flag him down. I was chairman of the racing committee then and we didn't want the track all cut up in the rain. We'd have a real bad time packing it all down again if he cut it up and so I tried to flag him and get him off there."

Who cares, thought McAllister, Dear Lord who the hell cares what happened forty-nine lousy years ago on some lousy dirt track in Missouri? He's failed at everything he ever tried in his life, lost all my mother's money, made her sell our house to invest in one of his crazy schemes and lived just as he wanted to live, not caring for what other people wanted, what my mother wanted, or me, or anyone. He's a failure and I hope to God I'm never like him. But to hear him talk you'd think he was a big, raging success at everything. From auto racing to raising chickens...I'll bet he never won a race in his life, Paul thought, never in his life.

"So he hits me," the old man was saying, his voice droning on in the heat, behind McAllister's thoughts. "He skidded, comes sideways across the wet track and hits me." The old man threw up a leathery hand. "Knocked me ten feet in the air and broke every bone in my body. Even today I got a plate in my left leg that aches when it rains." He tapped the spot. "Silver plate just like on a dinner table. Right here in my leg."

"Golly...that's something," said the boy from the rear seat. McAllister found it impossible to tell whether he was simply bored and being polite or whether he really wanted to hear more of this.

"They put me in the morgue. Left me for dead!" The old man nodded again, chuckling with a sound like wind in high grass. A rustling, repulsive kind of chuckle, thought McAllister.

"But I woke up and threw off that sheet and crawled across that cold floor to the feller in charge and scared him half to death. They took me to the hospital and I was out and walking in two weeks!"

Yes, and tell him about your fistula and your ulcers and the cancer you got over like it was a cold in the head, McAllister silently prodded. Tell him how you're stronger even than God in his heaven! Roosevelt dies and Stalin and Ronald Colman but you go right on. Not human, that's all; you're just not human.

"I drove the Pathfinder car for the Star Cup Tour back in 1910," the old man said. "That was in the Stevens-Duryea I mentioned. We called 'er the Big Six and she was sixty horsepower. Steering her was like grabbing a wagon wheel and it took a mile to get her rolling good. But then she'd do eighty. Roads were gumbo in those days. We couldn't get her movin' very fast on those roads. I had the agency for Stevens-Duryea in Kansas City then and I was selected over forty other dealers to blaze the way for the Star Cup runners. I mean, I drove the whole two thousand miles and we laid out the route for the auto tour that came later that year. We were the first car over the Glorietta mountains in New Mexico, first car to ever travel the Old Santa Fe trail." Paul's father was caught up afresh in the emotion of the Golden Era, and McAllister wondered where in hell that new gas station was, how many more miles they had to go before the kid could be dumped and the conversation terminated.

"Oh, we had ourselves a *time*," the old man chuckled. He needed a shave and the sun picked up the spiny edge of beard along his lower jaw. "Dust, gumbo, rocks so big it took the four of us to move 'em, rain and cold and roads like goat trails. Had ten rainstorms the first two and a half days out of Kansas City. But we made it, the whole way and back, and when we rolled into Kansas they tied wheat to the sides of the Big Six and we came on into Missouri, into Kansas City, and the crowds were out in the streets shouting at us and yelling our names…" The old man's voice dimmed away into memory.

"Didn't you have any breakdowns?" asked the boy.

"None major. We never missed an explosion in all the two thousand miles. I mean, the engine didn't. Ran like a clock. I tell you if cars ran like they used to they wouldn't need mechanics like you these days. Young buck like you could get out and hustle for work 'cuz there just wouldn't be none if the cars were all like my Big Six. Oh, we broke a wheel in the Gloriettas, but we got her changed quick enough. Had to use a mule team to haul us outa one big mudhole in Colorado but she never missed an explosion. No sir, she never missed."

Ahead of them, near a broad intersection, McAllister spotted the gas station. Thank God, he thought, for the sign of the Flying Red Horse! Never looked so good to me before. And just in time, too, or else he would have gone into the business of entering the Star Cup tour and leading most of the way and then breaking down near the end and the whole long bit. I couldn't take that, thought McAllister, as he approached the intersection, I just couldn't take that. A cream-colored Oldsmobile was moving rapidly out of the station and Paul had to twist the wheel and hardbrake to avoid him.

"Thanks, thanks a lot, mister," said the boy, jumping out and slamming the car door behind him. "And…" he hesitated, looking into the seamed face of the old man. "I sure do want to thank you for telling me about Barney Oldfield and all. I'll tell Al when I get back to L.A. and he'll have a fit he wasn't along. He'll just have himself a plain fit he didn't meet you."

They shook hands, Paul's father and the teenaged boy in blue denims—and just before the boy was about to turn away the old man raised an ivoried hand and gripped Paul's shoulder. "You see the way my boy handles this Ford? You see him whip it in here and miss that other feller? Handles this Ford like it was a kiddy car. Well, now, he drives, don't he? I watch him and I think of the way Wild Bob used to drive and I'm proud. Cuz he's just like him. My son here drives just like Wild Bob."

"I'll see ya," the boy said, and he waved as Paul rolled the car back onto the long flat highway.

"Nice youngster," the old man said, and he folded his bony arms across his chest. He coughed once and lapsed into silence.

In the mid-day heat, driving the tired Ford toward Los Angeles, Paul McAllister tried not to think about his father, or 1910, or a car named the Stevens-Duryea, or a man they called Wild Bob. And, most particularly, he tried not to think of the compliment his father had paid him, of the words and the pride behind the words. The old man had no business saying a thing like that and making him feel the way he suddenly felt. It threw everything out of perspective; it didn't fit the pattern.

I didn't ask him for it, McAllister thought angrily, I didn't *want* him to say it.

But the words of pride had been spoken and although McAllister gripped the wheel tighter and pressed harder on the gas pedal the rush of highway and the heat and his own inner voice telling him to forget, to ignore the words, failed. They failed to dull the sudden ache within his chest, the pain that stabbed at him from a place he could never hope to reach.

Beside him, sitting as straight as a soldier, his father produced the gray handkerchief and scrubbed at his watering eyes.

# THIRTY SEVEN 37

## CREATING AN ECHO:
### BE MEMORABLE

Effective fiction should leave the reader with something to think about after the final page has been turned. Something to ponder beyond the surface plot. Ideally, fiction should continue to reverberate within the psyche, permanently changing the reader's consciousness in an important—although often subtle—way.

I frequently attempt to incorporate something I call my *echo effect* into my fiction. Some examples will illustrate:

> • In my story "The Halloween Man" a schoolgirl becomes obsessed with a ghoul-creature—a stealer of souls—who, it is said, appears only on Halloween night. She convinces herself that the Halloween Man is real, and when her father (at the story's climax) attempts to calm her fears, she is suddenly sure that *he* is the fearsome creature.

But is he? Or is it all in her mind? At the end, the reader is left to ponder the Halloween Man's ultimate reality and I achieve my echo effect.

> • The character in my "Fair Trade" tells the sheriff about a grisly murder. He claims that *he* didn't do it, that he simply followed a newly risen corpse into town and watched the dead man commit the murder.

Is his statement to the sheriff the product of a deranged mind? (I *love* to write about deranged minds!) Or did the murder take place as described? I leave the answer to my readers.

• In *Logan's Run*, Jessica and Logan lift off for Sanctuary in a rocket, but will they make it there safely? And what will happen to them once they arrive? Will they have children? Will they ever return to Earth?

At the end of *Logan's Run*, these are questions for my readers to decide, but the echo effect was so strong in this novel that it subsequently generated three more adventures: *Logan's World, Logan's Search*, and *Logan's Return*.

Since the echo effect depends greatly on the shape and content of a particular story, not all of my fiction is designed to achieve it. But on those occasions when I can bring it off—when I am able to leave my readers with something to contemplate—I add this extra dimension of resonance to my work.

Try it.

You can do the same.

# Thirty Eight 38

## REVISION:
### How the Pros Do It

Congratulations! You have a completed draft. A new short story. You think it's pretty good but feel it's probably a bit too long, and there are several things you know need improving. So how do you proceed?

Start with the realization that virtually every first draft needs cutting.

• Begin with excessive description. (Do you really need *all* of it?)

• Check for extended dialogue. (Your characters should say only what is needed to advance the story.)

• Examine your sentences to see if they're overlong or flabby. (Can they be cut in half if you delete the nonessentials?)

• Examine each word in your story. Does that particular word convey exactly what you want to say? Every word has a weight of its own. Some words are too heavy for a particular placement; others are too light. Choose the *optimum* word. Use the latest hardback edition of *Roget's International Thesaurus*, the definitive thesaurus for writers, as well as the latest edition of Merriam-Webster's *New Collegiate Dictionary*, also the definitive reference source for most professional writers.

Every story I write goes through a predictable series of drafts. My first draft is handwritten. I revise it.

I then do a second draft on my typewriter. (I prefer to use a typewriter, though you'll probably use your PC.) I revise my typewritten draft.

Then I turn *that* draft over to my wife, author Cameron Nolan, who keyboards it into her computer as she simultaneously acts as my editor. She corrects any mistakes I may have made and catches anything I may have inadvertently missed. Then I correct *her* draft, and she keyboards the final revisions.

The pages which finally emerge from the computer printer are the ones I send out to market.

*Never* send a first draft to an editor, no matter how pleased you may be with it. Put it away for at least a week, perhaps more. Then reread your pages. Trust me, you'll find many ways to cut and improve your prose with each new draft.

Be objective about your work. Treat it as if someone else wrote it and then called you in as an outside authority to edit the manuscript. For example: you may be fond of details or elements that just don't belong in your story. These must be edited out.

Your job is to provide direct communication, writer to reader. Anything that impedes direct communication must be eliminated or rewritten.

Be ruthless in your quest for professionalism.

Get it right.

Revise your work until it is at its optimum.

It's the only way to become a real pro.

# V.

# WRITING SCREENPLAYS

# Thirty Nine 39

## SHIFTING GEARS:
### WRITING FOR HOLLYWOOD

In addition to prose writing, I have worked extensively in the film and television industry for some three-and-a-half decades.

Writing a screenplay or teleplay requires special techniques, and many established prose writers I know are unable to make the transition from story to script. The reverse is also true: many accomplished scriptwriters are incapable of writing prose. Fortunately, I have been able to function successfully in both areas. It's a matter of shifting gears, of moving to a different level of creativity.

But before I discuss the techniques of scriptwriting, I have a warning for those of you who wish to write for films or television: If you want to work "for Hollywood," it is essential that you reside within the greater Los Angeles area of California. For shows produced in New York, you must live within commuting distance of Manhattan, and Canadian writers must live near Vancouver or Toronto. Unless you're Stephen King, who resides in Maine, you simply cannot live in another geographical area and sell your scriptwriting talents to the entertainment industry. A producer or network executive may phone you late at night regarding a story conference early the next morning in the executive's office. If you aren't in town to personally pitch your story, or confer with the relevant development execs, you will not sell your wares. I know of only one writer (beyond King) who has been able to sell scripts to Hollywood without living in Los Angeles, and even he has to drive or fly south from his home in San Francisco for story conferences.

With that warning in mind, let's talk about scriptwriting.

When you're writing prose—novels and short stories—you're free to take your reader into the mind of your character. In scripts, this cannot be done. To put it simply: Prose is often interior writing, while scripts are virtually always exterior writing. (The exception is that, occasionally, voice-over narration is used in mainstream TV and film scripts, but this once popular technique of dramatic storytelling became passé some time ago.)

With scripts, you are limited to creating for the ear and the eye. In other words, you must confine yourself to what is capable of being recorded by microphone and camera. So far as script-writing is concerned, the inner thoughts, feelings, and motivations of your characters can be expressed *only* by means of spoken dialogue and action.

Scriptwriting is creativity stripped of its non-essentials. It must convey a great deal of information (including motivation and backstory) in very few words. Spoken dialogue must be brisk, crisp, and to the point. No lengthy verbal ruminations are allowed. Description is equally lean: a few words to set the scene; nothing more.

In prose writing, the mood of the piece and the emotional aura are the writer's creation. In film and television, however, these expressions are the purview of the director. The writer creates a written "recipe," but the actors and behind-the-camera personnel, following the director's vision, utilize that recipe only as a suggested blueprint during the production of the finished creation.

And please, avoid the classic beginning scriptwriter's mistake: Do *not* include camera directions! It is the *director's* responsibility to determine shots and camera angles. Including elaborate camera directions is the mark of the amateur, so keep your script simple and direct.

Script formatting is constantly evolving within the industry, and it often varies by the type of script (film script or teleplay, soap opera or TV sitcom, etc.). There are several brands of computer software and books describing and illustrating current script formatting on the market. See the Resources for Writers section at the back of this book.

My first script, in 1959, was written for the TV series *One Step Beyond*. It was a thirty-minute teleplay about a ghostly operation at sea. I followed that first sale with two scripts for Steve McQueen's *Wanted, Dead or Alive*, and I also wrote an episode of *240-Robert*. Most scriptwriters begin this way, with episodic television, gradually working up to the higher-paying movies made for television and, eventually, to screenplays.

In the early 1970s, when producer/director Dan Curtis moved from New York to Los Angeles after the highly successful run of his series *Dark Shadows*, he asked me to join his production staff. I turned him down, explaining that I wanted to *write* for him. This resulted in *The Norliss Tapes*, my Movie of the Week debut, which starred Angie Dickinson as the harassed wife of a walking dead man. *Norliss* was intended to be the pilot show for a proposed new TV series, but a subsequent strike by the Writers Guild of America killed the project.

Dan and I worked together over the next three years on a variety of film and TV dramas (including *Trilogy of Terror, Melvin Purvis, G-Man,* and *The Kansas City Massacre*). I adapted the classic Henry James ghost story, *The Turn of the Screw*, as a two-night TV miniseries which Dan filmed in London with Lynn Redgrave. Curtis and I also wrote what became one of the last Bette Davis films, *Burnt Offerings*.

Writing for films and television is often bizarre. I call it Alice-down-the-rabbit-hole. A scriptwriter needs a strong stomach, a tough hide, and an abiding sense of humor in order to survive in this mad industry.

Every veteran scripter has a personal collection of crazy Hollywood stories, and I'm no exception. A couple of my own are very much worth relating. Bear in mind that what I'm going to tell you actually happened exactly as described. (With these sorts of Hollywood stories, you don't need to fabricate or embellish. The truth is fantastic enough.)

In 1977 a producer at ABC asked me if I recalled the old Universal film version of *The Mummy*.

"Oh, sure," I said. "The one with Boris Karloff. A classic."

"Yeah, but it needs updating," said the producer. "We want to do a modern take on it, a jazzed-up version, and we think you're just the boy to write it."

"Sounds like fun," I said.

"Remember how ole Boris walked as the mummy?"

I nodded. "One arm held out, kind of shambling along, slowly."

"Too *damn* slow!" snapped the producer. "We don't want some drag-ass, shambling old guy in our flick. He has to really *move*. We want a powerful, fast mummy."

I nodded again.

"We want him to come to life, in this museum, after he gets zapped by some loose gamma rays."

"Gamma rays in a museum?" I queried.

He shrugged. "Do an outline first. We okay it, then you go to script."

"Gotcha," I said.

I set to work. The mummy is bombarded with gamma rays, comes to life, and runs amok in the San Fernando Valley of Los Angeles.

ABC liked my first outline, but had some "notes" (industry talk for changes). "We want him to kill a blonde. A real babe in a bikini. Maybe have her found in her swimming pool, dead as hell."

I revised the script to their specifications. At the next story conference I was asked: "How do we know that it was our guy who iced the blonde?"

I improvised. "The cops find a rotted strand of mummy wrapping floating next to the body."

"Brilliant," said the producer. "Absolutely brilliant." (In Hollywood, everything is either "lousy" or "brilliant.")

For the third revised outline they had a major change: because pyramid power was a hot topic at that time—though becoming passé—they wanted me to incorporate as much "pyramid power" as possible into the script.

"No sweat," I told them. I gave the cop-hero a pyramid-shaped refrigerator (according to those in the know, improved food preservation was one of the benefits of pyramid power), and I had him sit under a pyramid-shaped umbrella in his back yard. I was told my pyramid power additions were "brilliant."

And I made the mummy fast, strong, and powerful, as demonstrated in an action scene where a cop's car comes down an alley after the mummy, and the mummy pulls a heavy metal parking meter out of the concrete sidewalk (the way you'd pull a weed out of mud), then slams the meter into the cop's windshield. The patrol car goes out of control and smashes into a clothing store across the street. Hats fly everywhere.

"Brilliant," declared the producer.

Two months and three outlines later I was called in for a network meeting.

"We got good news and bad news," said the producer. "What do you want first?"

"The good news," I said.

"Good news is you got a go for scripting."

"Super," I said. "What's the bad news?"

"We need you to make one more change."

"Hey," I smiled. "No problem. I'm Mr. Elastic. Been making changes for *months*. No sweat. What do you want me to do?"

"Drop the mummy," he said.

I stared at him, jaw agape. "You mean like do *King Kong* without the ape?"

He smiled broadly. "See, it's a cinch." His voice rose in pitch. "We don't *need* the damn mummy. All we need is the *curse*. We're going to call it *The Curse of the Mummy*."

I swallowed, still staring at him.

"We have five characters break into the old guy's tomb in the first act and then they start kickin' off, one-by-one. In the final act, when the last of 'em goes belly up, we do a voice-over: 'Did they die by accident? Or was it The Curse of the Mummy?' And then we plant this big red question mark on the screen." He sat back in his swivel chair, looking satisfied. "Whatd'ya think?"

"I think I'm leaving," I said. And I walked.

(Needless to say, *The Curse of the Mummy* was never produced.)

Later that same year I took a phone call from David Greene, a producer at MGM. He told me CBS was hot to do an original Movie of the Week with a hero based directly on the fictional character of Zorro. Was I interested in taking at shot at it?

I sure was.

"They don't want to *call* him Zorro," said Greene (Zorro was the copyrighted character of author Johnston McCulley). "But they want him to wear a mask, just like Zorro, he's got to use a sword, and he must have a mute Indian companion. And he rides a great black stallion, like Mr. Z did."

"Got it," I said.

"They're in a big rush on this one," Greene said. "You can skip the outline and go right into script."

I set to work on a hero I called "The Nighthawk" who slashes an "N"—rather than a "Z"—into walls and doors with his sword. I gave him a mask, a mute Indian companion, and a big, black horse. My teleplay was titled *The Nighthawk Rides*.

"Brilliant," said Greene. "The network will love it. I'll have it messengered right over. You should hear by the weekend."

But I didn't. A full month went by, and I heard zilch.

Frustrated, I finally phoned Greene's office at MGM. "How come I haven't heard from the network?"

"Well," he said, "they thought your script was brilliant." His tone darkened. "However…"

"However?" I prompted.

"They passed. They are not going to produce it."

"Why?"

Greene sighed. "They say it's too much like Zorro."

And that's Hollywood.

In all, I wrote two dozen Movies of the Week for television, but just nine of them were produced. Actually, this is a very high percentage, since on average only one in ten completed teleplays ever goes before the cameras. The shelves at network and studio offices are jammed with written (and often paid for) unproduced scripts.

Everyone seems to want to write for Hollywood, which is fine so long as you realize the massive odds against you. Without a savvy, aggressive agent, and unless you live within an hour's drive (via congested freeways) from the studios and networks, forget it.

For you, it's better to stick to prose.

# ADAPTING 'THE PARTY':
## SHORT STORY TO SCRIPT

My short story "The Party" was originally printed in the April 1967 issue of *Playboy*. It was subsequently chosen for five anthologies including *Great Tales of Horror and the Supernatural*, reprinted in a Belgian magazine, adapted for radio, illustrated in comic-book format, and offered as a download on the Internet. I have included "The Party" in five of my short fiction collections and in October of 1991 I was delighted and stunned when *Newsweek* selected it as one of the seven outstanding horror tales of the twentieth century. There it was, short-listed among such classics as "The Monkey's Paw" by W. W. Jacobs and Saki's "The Open Window."

When I was asked to adapt this story for television, as part of the *Darkroom* series on ABC, I added new "bookend" material to my script, provided my protagonist with a pair of dead wives, and altered the climax. I made every effort to retain as much of the story's original dialogue as possible.

I'm presenting both versions of "The Party" here, in order to demonstrate how a prose story can be converted to a script format. Short story and teleplay appear here, together for the first time within a single book.

Study them both—and you'll see how it's done.

## The Party (short story version)

Ashland frowned, trying to concentrate in the warm emptiness of the thickly carpeted lobby. Obviously, he had pressed the elevator button, because he was alone here and the elevator was blinking its way down to him, summoned from an upper floor. It arrived with an efficient hiss, the bronze doors clicked open, and he stepped in, thinking blackout. I had a mental blackout.

First the double vision. Now this. It was getting worse. Just where the hell was he? Must be a party, he told himself. Sure. Someone he'd met, whose name was missing along with the rest of it, had invited him to a party. He had an apartment number in his head: 9E. That much he retained. A number—nothing else.

On the way up, in the soundless cage of the elevator, David Ashland reviewed the day. The usual morning routine: work, then lunch with his new secretary. A swinger—but she liked her booze; put away three martinis to his two. Back to the office. More work. A drink in the afternoon with a writer. ("Beefeater. No rocks. Very dry.") Dinner at the new Italian joint on West Forty-eighth with Linda. Lovely Linda. Expensive girl. Lovely as hell, but expensive. More drinks, then—nothing. Blackout.

The doc had warned him about the hard stuff, but what else can you do in New York? The pressures get to you, so you drink. Everybody drinks. And every night, somewhere in town, there's a party, with contacts (and girls) to be made...

The elevator stopped, opened its doors. Ashland stepped out, uncertainly, into the hall. The softly lit passageway was long, empty, silent. No, not silent. Ashland heard the familiar voice of a party: the shifting hive hum of cocktail conversation, dim, high laughter, the sharp clatter of ice against glass, a background wash of modern jazz...all quite familiar. And always the same.

He walked to 9E. Featureless apartment door. White.

Brass button housing. Gold numbers. No clues here. Sighing, he thumbed the buzzer and waited nervously.

A smiling fat man with bad teeth opened the door. He was holding a half-filled drink in one hand. Ashland didn't know him.

"C'mon in, fella," he said. "Join the party."

Ashland squinted into blue-swirled tobacco smoke, adjusting his eyes to the dim interior. The rising-falling sea tide of voices seemed to envelop him.

"Grab a drink, fella," said the fat man. "Looks like you need one!"

Ashland aimed for the bar in one corner of the crowded apartment. He *did* need a drink. Maybe a drink would clear his head, let him get this all straight. Thus far, he had not recognized any of the faces in the smoke-hazed room.

At the self-service bar a thin, turkey-necked woman wearing paste jewelry was intently mixing a black Russian. "Got to be exceedingly careful with these," she said to Ashland, eyes still on the mixture. "Too much vodka craps them up."

Ashland nodded. "The host arrived?" *I'll know him, I'm sure.*

"Due later—or sooner. Sooner—or later. You know, I once spilled three black Russians on the same man over a thirty-day period. First on the man's sleeve, then on his back, then on his lap. Each time his suit was a sticky, gummy mess. My psychiatrist told me that I did it unconsciously, because of a neurotic hatred of this particular man. He looked like my father."

"The psychiatrist?"

"No, the man I spilled the Russians on." She held up the tall drink, sipped at it. "Ahhh…still too weak."

Ashland probed the room for a face he knew, but these people were all strangers.

He turned to find the turkey-necked woman staring at him. "Nice apartment," he said mechanically.

"Stinks. I detest pseudo-Chinese decor in Manhattan

brownstones." She moved off, not looking back at Ashland.

He mixed himself a straight Scotch, running his gaze around the apartment. The place was pretty wild: ivory tables with serpent legs; tall, figured screens with chain-mail warriors cavorting across them; heavy brocade drapes in stitched silver; lamps with jewel-eyed dragons looped at the base. And, at the far end of the room, an immense bronze gong suspended between a pair of demon-faced swordsmen. Ashland studied the gong. A thing to wake the dead, he thought. Great for hangovers in the morning.

"Just get here?" a girl asked him. She was red-haired, full-breasted, in her late twenties. Attractive. Damned attractive. Ashland smiled warmly at her.

"That's right," he said, "I just arrived." He tasted the Scotch; it was flat, watery. "Whose place is this?"

The girl peered at him above her cocktail glass. "Don't you know who invited you?"

Ashland was embarrassed. "Frankly, no. That's why I—"

"My name's Viv. For Vivian. I drink. What do you do? Besides drink?"

"I produce. I'm in television."

"Well, I'm in a dancing mood. Shall we?"

"Nobody's dancing," protested Ashland. We'd look – foolish."

The jazz suddenly seemed louder. Overhead speakers were sending out a thudding drum solo behind muted strings. The girl's body rippled to the sounds.

"Never be afraid to do anything foolish," she told him. "That's the secret of survival." Her fingers beckoned him. "C'mon…"

"No, really—not right now. Maybe later."

"Then I'll dance alone."

She spun into the crowd, her long red dress whirling. The other party-goers ignored her. Ashland emptied the watery Scotch and fixed himself another. He loosened his tie, popping the collar button. *Damn!*

"I train worms."

Ashland turned to a florid-faced little man with bulging, feverish eyes. "I heard you say you were in TV," the little man said. "Ever use any trained worms on your show?"

"No...no, I haven't."

"I breed 'em, train 'em. I teach a worm to run a maze. Then I grind him up and feed him to a dumb, untrained worm. Know what happens? The dumb worm can run the maze! But only for twenty-four hours. Then he forgets—unless I keep him on a trained-worm diet. I defy you to tell me that isn't fascinating!"

"It is, indeed." Ashland nodded and moved away from the bar. The feverish little man smiled after him, toasting his departure with a raised glass. Ashland found himself sweating.

Who was his host? Who had invited him? He knew most of the Village crowd, but had spotted none of them here...

A dark, doll-like girl asked him for a light. He fumbled out some matches.

"Thanks," she said, exhaling blue smoke into blue smoke. "Saw that worm guy talking to you. What a lousy bore he is! My ex-husband had a pet snake named Baby and he fed it worms. That's all they're good for, unless you fish. Do you fish?"

"I've done some fishing up in Canada."

"My ex-husband hated all sports. Except the indoor variety." She giggled. "Did you hear the one about the indoor hen and the outdoor rooster?"

"Look, miss—"

"Talia. But you can call me Jenny. Get it?" She doubled over, laughing hysterically, then swayed, dropping her cigarette. "Ooops! I'm sick. I better go lie down. My tum-tum feels awful."

She staggered from the party as Ashland crushed out her smoldering cigarette with the heel of his shoe. *Stupid bitch!*

A sharp handclap startled him. In the middle of the room, a tall man in a green satin dinner jacket was demanding his attention. He clapped again. "You," he shouted to Ashland. "Come here."

Ashland walked forward. The tall man asked him to remove his wristwatch. "I'll read your past from it," the man said. "I'm psychic. I'll tell you about yourself."

Reluctantly, Ashland removed his watch, handed it over. He didn't find any of this amusing. The party was annoying him, irritating him.

"I thank you most kindly, sir!" said the tall man, with elaborate stage courtesy. He placed the gold watch against his forehead and closed his eyes, breathing deeply. The crowd noise did not slacken; no one seemed to be paying any attention to the psychic.

"Ah. Your name is David. David Ashland. You are successful, a man of big business…a producer…and a bachelor. You are twenty-eight…young for a successful producer. One has to be something of a bastard to climb that fast. What about that, Mr. Ashland, *are* you something of a bastard?"

Ashland flushed angrily.

"You like women," continued the tall man. "A lot. And you like to drink. A lot. Your doctor told you—"

"I don't have to listen to this," Ashland said tightly, reaching for his watch. The man in green satin handed it over, grinned amiably, and melted back into the shifting crowd.

I ought to get the hell out of here, Ashland told himself. Yet curiosity held him. When the host arrived, Ashland would piece this evening together; he'd know why he was here, at this particular party. He moved to a couch near the closed patio doors and sat down. He'd wait.

A soft-faced man sat down next to him. The man looked pained. "I shouldn't smoke these," he said, holding up a long cigar. "Do you smoke cigars?"

"No."

"I'm a salesman. Dover Insurance. Like the White Cliffs of, ya know. I've studied the problems involved in smoking. Can't quit, though. When I do, the nerves shrivel up, stomach goes sour. I worry a lot—but we all worry, don't we? I mean, my mother used to worry about the earth slowing down. She read somewhere that between 1680 and 1690 the earth lost twenty-seven hundredths of a second. She said that meant something."

Ashland sighed inwardly. What is it about cocktail parties that causes people you've never met to unleash their troubles?

"You meet a lotta fruitcakes in my dodge," said the pained-looking insurance salesman. "I sold a policy once to a guy who lived in the woodwork. Had a ratty little walk-up in the Bronx with a foldaway bed. Kind you push into the wall. He'd *stay* there—I mean inside the wall—most of the time. His roommate would invite some friends in and if they made too much noise the guy inside the wall would pop out with this Thompson. BAM! The bed would come down and there he was with a Thompson submachine gun aimed at everybody. Real fruitcake."

"I knew a fellow who was *twice* that crazy."

Ashland looked up into a long, cadaverous face. The nose had been broken and improperly reset; it canted noticeably to the left. He folded his long, sharp-boned frame onto the couch next to Ashland. "This fellow believed in falling grandmothers," he declared. "Lived in upper Michigan. 'Watch out for falling grandmothers,' he used to warn me. 'They come down pretty heavy in this area. Most of 'em carry umbrellas and big packages and they come flapping down out of the sky by the thousands.' This Michigan fellow swore he saw one hit a postman. 'An awful thing to watch,' he told me. 'Knocked the poor soul flat. Crushed his skull like an egg.' I recall he shuddered just telling me about it."

"Fruitcake," said the salesman. "Like the guy I once knew who wrote on all his walls and ceilings. A creative writer, he called himself. Said he couldn't write on paper, had to use a wall. Paper was too flimsy for him. He'd scrawl these long novels of his, a chapter in every room, with a big black crayon. Words all over the place. He'd fill up the house, then rent another one for his next book. I never read any of his houses, so I don't know if he was any good."

"Excuse me, gentlemen," said Ashland. "I need a fresh drink."

He hurriedly mixed another Scotch at the bar. Around him, the party rolled on inexorably, without any visible core. What time was it, anyway? His watch had stopped.

"Do you happen to know what time it is?" he asked a long-haired Oriental girl who was standing near the bar.

"I've no idea," she said. "None at all." The girl fixed him with her eyes. "I've been watching you, and you seem horribly *alone*. Aren't you?"

"Aren't I what?"

"Horribly alone?"

"I'm not with anyone, if that's what you mean."

The girl withdrew a jeweled holder from her bag and fitted a cigarette in place. Ashland lit it for her.

"I haven't been really alone since I was in Milwaukee," she told him. "I was about—God!—fifteen or something, and this creep wanted me to move in with him. My parents were both dead by then, so I was all alone."

"What did you do?"

"Moved in with the creep. What else? I couldn't make the being-alone scene. Later on, I killed him."

"You what?"

"Cut his throat." She smiled delicately. "In self-defense, of course. He got mean on the bottle one Friday night and tried to knife me. I had witnesses."

Ashland took a long draw on his Scotch. A scowling fellow in shirt sleeves grabbed the girl's elbow and steered her roughly away.

"I used to know a girl who looked like that," said a voice to Ashland's right. The speaker was curly-haired, clean-featured, in his late thirties. "Greek belly dancer with a Jersey accent. Dark, like her, and kind of mysterious. She used to quote that line of Hemingway's to Scott Fitzgerald—you know the one."

"Afraid not."

"One that goes, 'We're all bitched from the start.' Bitter. A bitter line."

He put out his hand. Ashland shook it.

"I'm Travers. I used to save America's ass every week on CBS."

"Beg pardon?"

"Terry Travers. The old *Triple Trouble for Terry* series on channel nine. Back in the late fifties. Had to step on a lotta toes to get that series."

"I think I recall the show. It was—"

"Dung. That's what it was. Cow dung. Horse dung. The *worst*. Terry Travers is not my real name, natch. Real one's Abe Hockstatter. Can you imagine a guy named Abe Hockstatter saving America's ass every week on CBS?"

"You've got me there."

Hockstatter pulled a brown wallet from his coat, flipped it open. "There I am with one of my other rugs on," he said, jabbing at a photo. "Been stone bald since high school. Baldies don't make it in showbiz, so I have my rugs. Go ahead, tug at me."

Ashland blinked. The man inclined his head. "*Pull* at it. Go on—as a favor to me!"

Ashland tugged at the fringe of Abe Hockstatter's curly hairpiece.

"Tight, huh? Really *snug*. Stays on the old dome."

"Indeed it does."

"They cost a fortune. I've got a wind-blown one for outdoor scenes. A stiff wind'll lift a cheap one right off your scalp. Then I got a crew cut and a Western job with long sideburns. All kinds. Ten, twelve...all first-class."

"I'm certain I have seen you," said Ashland. "I just don't—"

"S'awright. Believe me. Lotta people don't know me since I quit the *Terry* thing. I booze like crazy now. You an' me, we're among the nation's six million alcoholics."

Ashland glared at the actor. "Where do you get off linking me with—"

"Cool it, cool it. So I spoke a little out of turn. Don't be so touchy, chum."

"To hell with you!" snapped Ashland.

The bald man with curly hair shrugged and drifted into the crowd.

Ashland took another long pull at his Scotch. All these neurotic conversations…He felt exhausted, wrung dry, and the Scotch was lousy. No kick to it. The skin along the back of his neck felt tight, hot. A headache was coming on; he could always tell.

A slim-figured, frosted blonde in black sequins sidled up to him. She exuded an aura of matrimonial wars fought and lost. Her orange lipstick was smeared, her cheeks alcohol-flushed behind flaking pancake make-up. "I have a theory about sleep," she said. "Would you like to hear it?"

Ashland did not reply.

"My theory is that the world goes insane every night. When we sleep, our subconscious takes charge and we become victims to whatever it conjures up. Our conscious mind is totally blanked out. We lie there, helpless, while our subconscious flings us about. We fall off high buildings, or have to fight a giant ape, or we get buried in quicksand…We have absolutely no control. The mind whirls madly in the skull. Isn't that an unsettling thing to consider?"

"Listen," said Ashland. "Where's the host?"

"He'll get here."

Ashland put down his glass and turned away from her. A mounting wave of depression swept him toward the door. The room seemed to be solid with bodies, all talking, drinking, gesturing in the milk-thick smoke haze.

"Potatoes have eyes," said a voice to his left. "I really believe that." The remark was punctuated by an ugly, frog-croaking laugh.

"Today is tomorrow's yesterday," someone else said.

A hot swarm of sound.

"You can't get prints off human skin."

"In China, the laborers make sixty-five dollars a year. How the hell can you live on sixty-five dollars a year?"

"So he took out his Luger and blew her head off."

"I knew a policewoman who loved to scrub down whores."

"Did you ever try to live with eight kids, two dogs, a three-legged cat and twelve goldfish?"

"Like I told him, those X-rays destroyed his white cells."

"They found her in the tub. Strangled with a coat hanger."

"What I had, exactly, was a grade-two epidermoid carcinoma at the base of a seborrheic keratosis."

Ashland experienced a sudden, raw compulsion: somehow he had to stop these voices!

The Chinese gong flared gold at the corner of his eye. He pushed his way over to it, shouldering the party-goers aside. He would strike it—and the booming noise would stun the crowd; they'd have to stop their incessant, maddening chatter.

Ashland drew back his right fist, then drove it into the circle of bronze. He felt the impact, and the gong shuddered under his blow.

*But there was no sound from it!*

The conversation went on.

Ashland smashed his way back across the apartment.

"You can't stop the party," said the affable fat man at the door.

"I'm leaving!"

"So go ahead," grinned the fat man. "Leave."

Ashland clawed open the door and plunged into the hall, stumbling, almost falling. He reached the elevator, jabbed at the DOWN button.

Waiting, he found it impossible to swallow; his throat was dry. He could feel his heart hammering against the wall of his chest. His head ached.

The elevator arrived, opened. He stepped inside. The doors closed smoothly and the cage began its slow, automatic descent.

Abruptly, it stopped.

The doors parted to admit a solemn-looking man in a dark blue suit.

Ashland gasped. "Freddie!"

The solemn face broke into a wide smile. "Dave! It's great to see you! Been a long time."

"But—you can't be Fred Baker."

"Why? Have I changed so much?"

"No, no, you look—exactly the same. But that car crash in Albany. I thought you were…" Ashland hesitated, left the word unspoken. He was pale, frightened. Very frightened. "Look, I'm—I'm late. Got somebody waiting for me at my place. Have to rush…" He reached to push the LOBBY button.

There was none.

The lowest button read FLOOR 2.

"We use this elevator to get from one party to another," Freddie Baker said quietly, as the cage surged into motion. "That's all it's good for. You get so you need a change. They're all alike, though—the parties. But you learn to adjust, in time."

Ashland stared at his departed friend. The elevator stopped.

"Step out," said Freddie. "I'll introduce you around. You'll catch on, get used to things. No sex here. And the booze is watered. Can't get stoned. That's the dirty end of the stick."

Baker took Ashland's arm, propelled him gently forward.

Around him, pressing in, David Ashland could hear familiar sounds: nervous laughter, ice against glass, muted jazz—and the ceaseless hum of cocktail voices.

Freddie thumbed a buzzer. A door opened.

The smiling fat man said, "C'mon in, fellas. Join the party."

## The Party (teleplay version)

*FADE IN:*

INT. LIMO *(moving)*—NIGHT

*A uniformed chauffeur,* SIDNEY, *is at the wheel—behind a rolled-up glass partition separating driver from passengers. In the back seat:* DAVID ASHLAND *and his attractive wife,* LYDIA.

*They ride in tight-faced, sullen silence. Then...*

LYDIA: Congratulations. As usual, you managed to make a total fool of yourself.

ASHLAND: I was being funny. I'm always funny at parties.

LYDIA: Do you actually think it's *funny* to pour a whisky sour all over the hostess…fight with her husband …get us thrown out of the party?

ASHLAND: [*amused tone*]: Spilling the drink was an accident. I was trying to climb up on the piano. To sing. Very funny song.

*And he begins humming the melody.*

LYDIA [*acidly*]: Your songs are vulgar and disgusting.

ASHLAND [*suddenly angry*]: I'll tell you what's vulgar and disgusting—the way you went after that guitar player.

LYDIA: I have to find affection somewhere. God knows *you* don't supply it.

ASHLAND: You get what you give out in this world, sweetie. And you're a mighty cold fish.

*Another silence. Then she turns to him, looks him directly in the eye.*

LYDIA: How can you expect anything *but* coldness?…This kind of life…it killed your first wife.

ASHLAND: Trish drank herself to death. You know that

as well as I do. [*beat*] I can handle my booze. She couldn't.

LYDIA: You pushed her over the edge, David! She kept drinking more all the time, just to keep from going crazy— the same way *I* do. For all the same reasons.

ASHLAND [*in a cutting tone*]: Don't give me that! You drink because you like it. Nobody puts a gun to your head.

*More silence between them. She is beyond anger; she's made a decision.*

LYDIA [*calmly*]: David, I'm going to divorce you.

ASHLAND: Fine. Okay, okay. I don't need you. I never did.

LYDIA: No, all you need is another party, another vodka martini, another crowd to play the fool for.

ASHLAND: Look…if you want a divorce you've *got* it. With my blessing. But just shut up about what I need.

EXT. LIMO—THE STREET—NIGHT

*as it swings off the street onto a freeway ramp. Moves up the ramp and begins to enter the freeway through a swirl of ground fog.*

*There is the sudden, stabbing SOUND of a truck's* air-horn. *The limo has veered into the path of a giant truck/ trailer rig…*

INT. LIMO

*as* ASHLAND *pounds at the glass partition with the heel of one hand.*

ASHLAND [*shouting*]: Sidney! *Look out!*

*We see* SIDNEY *wrench the wheel violently left, and the limo begins sliding on the damp asphalt…*

EFFECT: *we are into a* wall *of fog, totally opaque. It forms a milk-white envelope around the limo.*

ASHLAND [*to Lydia*]: Can't see a damn thing out there!

*They suddenly emerge from the fog-wall into clear night air.* SIDNEY *rolls down the glass a few inches.*

SIDNEY: Sorry about that, Mr. Ashland. My fault en- tirely.

ASHLAND *nods, does not reply. He settles back into the seat as* SIDNEY *rolls the glass back up between them.*

LYDIA: That was close.

EXT. ASHLAND HOME—*FULL SHOT*—NIGHT

*as the black limo rolls smoothly up the circular, pebbled drive to the front entrance. The place is more than a house; it's a mansion.*

*ANGLE NEAR ENTRANCE*

*as* SIDNEY *stops the car, gets out to open the rear door for the* ASHLANDS. (He is, by the way, a "proper" chauffeur, in snappy cap and uniform.)

ASHLAND *steps out, but* LYDIA *does not.*

ASHLAND: Aren't you coming?

LYDIA: No—I'm going.

ASHLAND: Where?

LYDIA: Away from you. To my sister's maybe. Or downtown. I'll let you know. I just *don't* feel like going inside that house with you tonight.

ASHLAND: What about the car?

LYDIA: Sidney will bring it back after he's dropped me off.

ASHLAND: Suit yourself. I'm going in and have a drink.

LYDIA [*cynically*]: Now where have I heard that line before?

*And she leans forward to tap the glass.* SIDNEY *puts the car into gear.*

THE SCENE—WIDE SHOT

ASHLAND *stands in the entrance, watching the big car motor off into the darkness.*

INT. HOUSE—NIGHT

*as he enters, CAMERA WITH HIM. He tosses aside his topcoat, walks in cold anger down a long hallway, to:*

INT. LIBRARY/DEN—FIRELIGHT

ASHLAND *switches on a lamp, moves to the bar, pours himself a stiff shot.*

*ANGLE AT FIREPLACE*

*as he settles into a deep chair by the hearth, takes a long swallow from his glass. The flames play across his face as he nods to himself.*

ASHLAND: Have it your way, sweetie. Ole David here will make out just *fine* without you.

*And he watches the fire-patterns as we*

*DISSOLVE TO:*

*CLOSE ON* DOOR BUZZER (ASHLAND'S)— NIGHT

*as a finger presses it. PULL BACK TO:*

EXT. HOUSE—ON SIDNEY

*as he rings the bell once again. (The limo is parked on the driveway behind him in b.g.)*

*The door opens.* ASHLAND, *a half-filled glass in his hand, blinks out at his chauffeur.*

ASHLAND: What is it, Sidney? [*noticing the limo*] Why isn't the car in the garage?

SIDNEY: I thought you might wish to use it, sir.

ASHLAND: *Use* it! [*checks his wrist*] It's after three in the morning!

SIDNEY *removes a small white envelope from his uniform pocket.*

SIDNEY: Mrs. Ashland wants you to join her. [*hands over envelope*] This is for you, sir.

*CLOSE ON NOTE*

*as* ASHLAND *opens the envelope, unfolds the single white sheet. It reads:*

David—

Please forgive me for my wretched behavior tonight. I didn't really mean what I said to you. Guess I just had too much to drink.

I'm sending Sidney back to fetch you to this marvelous party I discovered. You'll adore it!

See you there, darling!

L.

*WIDER ON SCENE*

*as* ASHLAND *looks up from the note, puzzled.*

ASHLAND: Is she serious?

SIDNEY: Quite, sir. Mrs. Ashland asked me to drive you to the party.

ASHLAND [*with a what-the-hell smile*]: Well…I've never turned down one yet.

*DISSOLVE TO:*

INT. LIMO (*moving*)—NIGHT

*as the big car glides through the city.* ASHLAND *has rolled down the glass.*

ASHLAND: So, whose house are we headed for?…the Nalbins? Sterns? I hear the Kendricks are back from Monte Carlo…is it their place?

SIDNEY: No, sir. The party is downtown.

ASHLAND [*startled*]: I don't know anybody downtown!

SIDNEY: It's a new apartment building…That's all I can tell you, sir.

ASHLAND [*with a grin*]: You're being very mysterious, Sidney.

SIDNEY: Mrs. Ashland wants to surprise you, sir. I'm just doing as she asked.

ASHLAND *settles back with a contented sigh.*

ASHLAND: All right…I'm always game for a surprise. [*beat*] Drive on, McDuff!

*CUT TO:*

EXT. DOWNTOWN APARTMENT BUILDING—
*FULL*—NIGHT

*as the black limo pulls up to a tall, 20-story structure of shining glass. On the dark, fog-shrouded avenue, the building glows with a thousand lights from as many windows.*

SIDNEY *opens the door for* ASHLAND, *who emerges, looks up.*

*HIS POV—THE BUILDING*

*rising above him like an immense, bright-lit Christmas tree.*

BACK TO SCENE

*as* ASHLAND *shakes his head.*

ASHLAND: Never saw *this* before!

SIDNEY: As I said, sir, it's a new building.

ASHLAND: Their electric bill must be a killer! [*beat*]

Where's the party? What floor?

    SIDNEY: It's in 10-E. [*gets back into limo*] Have a good time, Mr. Ashland.

    And the black car purrs away into the fog.

    INT. APT. BUILDING'S LOBBY—NIGHT

    *as* ASHLAND *enters the wide, ornate lobby. His footfalls are soundless against thick red carpet as he moves toward the elevator. He is quite alone in this part of the building; no doorman or guard.*

    AT ELEVATOR

    *He pushes the "Up" button, waits, humming to himself. (It is the same melody we heard him hum earlier in the limo—a "party" song.)*

    *The doors click open and he enters the cage.*

CUT TO:

    INT. 10TH FLOOR HALLWAY

    ASHLAND *steps out of the elevator, CAMERA FOLLOW-ING. He walks along the hall, checking door numbers—finds the correct one.*

    *CAMERA FEATURES "10-E"*

    *ON* ASHLAND *AT DOOR*

    *as he thumbs the buzzer. Through the door, we hear the SOUNDS of a party: the sea-tide of cocktail conversation, the tinkle of iced drinks, muted music from a stereo...*

    *The door is opened by a jolly-faced* FAT MAN.

    *CLOSE ON* FAT MAN

    *as his sweating moon face breaks into a smile of welcome.*

    FAT MAN: Hi, fella! C'mon in! Join the party!

    INT. PARTY SUITE—*FULL*

    *as* DAVID ASHLAND *enters past the* FAT MAN. *The main party area is large and crowded with a variety of guests, young and old. It is decorated in a Chinese motif—ivory tables with serpent legs; figured screens; heavy drapes in stitched silver; lamps with jewel-eyed dragons looped at their base—and, in the room's far end—an immense bronze gong suspended between a pair of demon-faced warriors.*

*ANGLE TIGHTENS*

*as a thin, garish, turkey-necked woman moves up to* ASHLAND. *She is the kind one finds in Florida resort hotels; heavy eyelashes, too much makeup.*

THIN WOMAN: Hello, there! My, but…*[staring at him]* you look just like a man I saw once, outside the library when I was a child. He was sitting on a little stone bench I remember… *[beat]*…and he had his throat cut.

*Disturbed,* ASHLAND *walks away from her, CAMERA FOLLOWING, to the bar along one side of the room.*

*ANGLE AT BAR*

*as he mixes himself a drink. An attractive, red-haired young lady,* VIVIAN, *turns to him from the bar.*

VIVIAN: My name's Viv. I drink.

ASHLAND: I'm looking for my wife. Maybe you've met her…Lydia Ashland?

VIVIAN: Sorry—but I never help husbands find their wives. *[with a little finger wave]* Bye, bye!

*And she whirls off into the crowd.*

*A fever-eyed man approaches him.*

HEALTH MAN: If you wish to maintain your health, you can't just stand there. Keep moving. Stay ahead of 'em. Stand still and they'll form their cloud.

*The man is in constant motion as he talks, shifting from one foot to the other, weaving his body like a boxer.*

ASHLAND: Who will?

HEALTH MAN: The germs. They form clouds around people. If you don't keep moving they gang up on you. Form a germ-cloud. Billions of 'em. They can cause flu. Ever had the flu?

ASHLAND: Of course. Everybody gets the flu…

HEALTH MAN *[with a smirk]*: That's cuz people don't keep moving. *[beat]* Better get trotting, fella!

*And he's gone.*

*TIGHT ON* ASHLAND

*as he reacts to something directly behind, touching him. He turns to confront:*

SNAKE MAN

*Dressed in black, with a live snake curling round his waist and neck. He smiles at* ASHLAND.

SNAKE MAN: Her name's "Baby"…She likes to rub her head against your neck. Hope you're not afraid of snakes.

ASHLAND [*obviously repelled*]: I…uh…can't say that I'm fond of them.

SNAKE MAN: She's really very loving. Want to hold her?

ASHLAND [*moving off into the crowd*]: No…no thanks…

*CAMERA FOLLOWS HIM through the smoke-hazed room as he continues to look for* LYDIA. *Now, suddenly he sees:*

*HIS POV*

*a figure, from the back, who looks like* LYDIA *(same dress and hair). The woman leaves the main party area and starts toward the kitchen.*

*ON* ASHLAND

*as he attempts to follow, calling to her.*

ASHLAND: Lydia!

*CUT TO:*

INT. KITCHEN

*as* ASHLAND *enters quickly, INTO CAMERA. The room is full of partygoers—but no* LYDIA.

ASHLAND *approaches a bearded man near the door.*

ASHLAND: My wife just came in here…tall, in a green dress…did you see where she went?

WORM MAN: I no longer look at women. Can't do anything *with* them, so why look at them? [*beat*] I'm a worm trainer.

ASHLAND *is startled.*

ASHLAND: Beg pardon?

WORM MAN: I train a worm to run a maze. Then I grind him up and feed him to a dumb, untrained worm. Know what happens? [*beat*] The dumb worm can run the maze. But only for 24 hours. Then he forgets. Unless I keep him on a trained-worm diet. I *defy* you to tell me that isn't fascinating!

ASHLAND [*nods*]: It's fascinating—but right now I'm looking for my wife.

WORM MAN [with a chuckle]: And I'm looking for a way out of this kitchen!

ASHLAND, *sweating a bit now, somewhat harried, edges toward the back door of the kitchen, still searching for* LYDIA.

*A dark, doll-like girl (who could be a teenager) suddenly steps in front of him to hold out a cigarette.*

BLACK GIRL: Light?

*He fumbles out his silver lighter, applies flame to her cigarette. She takes a drag, blows the smoke out through her nose.*

BLACK GIRL: You seem *alone*. Are you? Alone, I mean.

ASHLAND [*putting away the lighter*]: No…my wife's here somewhere.

BLACK GIRL: I haven't been alone since Milwaukee. I was about 14 or something and this creep moves in with me. My parents were dead by then.

ASHLAND [*not sure what to say*]: I'm sorry.

BLACK GIRL: Yeah, this creep was sorry, too. Things were bad right from the start between us. That's why I killed him.

ASHLAND: You *what*?

BLACK GIRL: Shot him. Three times. [*she points a finger at* Ashland, *like a gun*] Bang! Bang! Bang! [*shrugs*] It was self-defense. He came at me with an iron golf club. He was a golfer.

ASHLAND: I'd better try and find my wife.

*But as he turns away from her, a curly-haired man grabs his arm.*

TRAVERS: I lost a wife once. Greek belly dancer with a Jersey accent. She used to quote that line of Hemingway's to Scott Fitzgerald—you know the line?"

ASHLAND: No, I—

TRAVERS: One that goes, "We're all bitched from the start." Bitter. Bitter line [*puts out his hand*] I'm Terry Travers. Not my real name, but no matter. Remember the ole *Triple*

*Trouble for Terry* series on TV?

ASHLAND: Not that I can recall.

TRAVERS: Had to step on a few people to get that series…[*flips open a wallet, showing a snapshot*] Lookie here, that's me before I did the show.

*CLOSE ON WALLET PHOTO*

TRAVERS, totally bald.

*BACK TO SCENE*

*as* ASHLAND *nods.*

TRAVERS: I wear rugs now. Have ever since the series. Top quality. Hand-sewn. [*inclines his head down*] Go ahead, *tug* at it.

ASHLAND: No, really, I'll take your word that—

TRAVERS: Aw, c'mon—as a personal favor to me. Tug at it.

ASHLAND *does, but without enthusiasm.*

TRAVERS [*note of pride*]: Snug, eh? Stays on the ole dome. I've got a wind-blown one for outdoor scenes. Then I got me a crewcut for Army-Navy flicks—and a western job with long sideburns. Absolutely authentic.

ASHLAND: I see.

TRAVERS: But I don't act anymore. I just booze. Me an' six million alcoholics!

ASHLAND: My wife's obviously not here. Guess I was mistaken about seeing her.

TRAVERS: It's all illusion. Reality versus illusion. Like they say, "A lie often reveals truth, but the truth is often a lie."

*Having had enough,* ASHLAND *leaves the kitchen.*

MAIN PARTY AREA

*as* ASHLAND *exits the kitchen he reacts to:*

VOICE (Psychic's) O.S.: You! You leaving the kitchen!

*HIS POV*

*a tall man in a satin dinner jacket with dark, intense eyes, standing atop a chair in the middle of the smoke-filled room.*

PSYCHIC [*gestures at ashland*]: Please, sir…a moment

of your time.

*ON SCENE*

*as* ASHLAND *moves warily through the crowd to the psychic.*

ASHLAND: You want me?

PSYCHIC [*extending a hand, fingers out*]: Might I borrow that ring you're wearing?

ASHLAND: Well, I really don't—

PSYCHIC: No harm will come to it, sir…If you please…

*Reluctantly,* ASHLAND *removes his wedding band, hands it up to the man on the chair.*

PSYCHIC [*cupping his hands around the ring, pressing his hands to his forehead*]:

Ah…now…let me begin to read the vibrations. [*beat*] Your first name begins with a "D"…not Daniel…or Dexter…Ah! David. Am I correct?

ASHLAND: That's right.

PSYCHIC: You are talented…an architect…and rich…However—you have not worked for your money. It's your father's money…a large inheritance.

ASHLAND'S *face is tight; he does not find this amusing.*

PSYCHIC [*continuing*]: You like women…and have married two of them…[*beat*] And you like to drink. Too much. Far, far too much.

ASHLAND *is now angry.*

ASHLAND: That's enough! [*thrusts up a hand*] My ring!

*The smiling psychic hands the ring back to him—and* ASHLAND *stalks away to the bar, CAMERA FOLLOWING.*

AT BAR

*where he mixes himself another scotch…sits down with the drink on a long couch, his face red and sweating.*

*Note: During the entire exchange with the psychic, few if any people paid the slightest attention to it.*

*ANGLE AT COUCH—TWO SHOT*

*as a soft-faced man seats himself very close to* ASHLAND.

SALESMAN: Do you worry a lot? I do. Runs in the family, I guess. Mother used to worry about the Earth slowing down. She read somewhere that between 1680 and 1690 the Earth lost 27/100ths of a second of its orbital speed. [*beat*] She said that was a bad sign.

ASHLAND: Don't mean to be rude, but frankly I'd rather not talk right now.

SALESMAN: So don't talk. *I'll* do the talking. Talk's my business. I'm a salesman. Dover Insurance. Like the White Cliffs of, ya know? [*beat*] Meet a lot of fruitcakes in this game. I sold a policy once to a guy who lived in the wood-work—spent all his time inside this foldaway bed in the wall. Had a real bad temper. Didn't care for many people. [*beat*] Well, one night his roommate invited some friends over and their noise woke up this guy—and out he pops from his bed in the wall with a loaded Thompson submachine gun in his hands, yelling for them all to get the hell out of his apartment. He was ready to cut loose with the Thompson.

ASHLAND: That's crazy.

THIN MAN'S VOICE (O.S.): I knew a man who was twice that crazy.

*ANGLE WIDENS to include a third man who has taken a seat on the other side of* ASHLAND *(also very close to him). He is incredibly thin, practically a walking cadaver.*

THIN MAN: This fellow lived up in Vermont, and he believed in falling grandmothers. [*beat*] "Watch out for falling grandmothers," he used to warn me. "They come down pretty heavy during winter in this area. Most of 'em carry umbrellas and big packages and come flapping down out of the sky by the thousands." [*another beat*] This Vermont guy swore he saw a postal worker killed by one. "Awful thing to watch," he told me. "Knocked him flat. Crushed his head like an eggshell."

*Before* ASHLAND *can react to this bit of madness, the salesman cuts right in:*

SALESMAN: Fruitcake! I know the kind. Like the guy I met who called himself a creative writer. Said he couldn't write on paper. Not enough texture. So he'd rent a house and scrawl these novels of his on walls and ceilings with a big black crayon, a chapter in every room. When he'd finish the novel he'd rent another house for the next one.

THIN MAN: Did he have talent?

SALESMAN [*with a shrug*]: Dunno. I never read any of his houses.

ASHLAND *stands up; his glass is empty again.*

ASHLAND: I have to get another drink.

THIN MAN [*raising his own glass*]: Booze is no good here…no damn good at all.

With a tight smile, ASHLAND moves away from them, back to the bar.

*ANGLE AT BAR*

*Now a frost-haired blonde in sequins edges up to* ASHLAND.

BLONDE: I have a theory about sleep. Would you care to hear it?

ASHLAND: Not particularly.

BLONDE [*charging on*]: My theory is that we all go insane each night. When we sleep our subconscious takes control—and we become unwilling victims to whatever it conjures up. Our conscious mind is totally out of it. We lie there, helpless, while our subconscious pushes us off high buildings, in front of speeding trains, buries us in quicksand…We have absolutely no control as the mind whirls madly in the skull. [*beat*] Isn't that unsettling to think about?

ASHLAND: Very. Now, if you'll excuse me—

*But she grips his arm, tightly.*

BLONDE: I wrote a poem about it…[*begins to recite*]: "In the skulled winding sheet / of our blooded nightmares / We sand-crawl / the hallways of madness!"

ASHLAND: I need to find my wife…I know she's here somewhere, and I—

*The* BLONDE *is relentless; she simply won't let him leave.*

BLONDE [*intense, her face close to his*]: You know, sometimes, even when you're awake, your mind can play awful tricks on you. Like…this one morning when I was in bed. Woke up. And here's this huge kind of spider-thing. And I mean it was huge! About the size of a baby… It was right there in bed with me…Well, you can *imagine* what I—

ASHLAND [*cutting her off*]: If you'll excuse me, I need to find my wife. She's here at the party.

*A hand touches his shoulder.* ASHLAND *swings around, facing:*

SIDNEY

*The chauffeur has his jacket off, shirt unbuttoned.*

SIDNEY: Looking for Mrs. Ashland?

ASHLAND *is startled.*

ASHLAND: Sidney! What are you—

SIDNEY: —doing at the party? [*he smiles*] I was invited. We were all invited.

ASHLAND: Where's my wife?

SIDNEY [*casually*]: Around. You'll run into her. Don't sweat it.

ASHLAND [*angry*]: Damn you! Where *is* she?

SIDNEY *does not answer. He turns away, walks into the depths of the crowd.*

*Note: More and more people have been entering the main party room and it is now jammed.*

*CAMERA WITH* ASHLAND

*as, really pissed, he goes after* SIDNEY—*and is literally engulfed in the crowd.*

*We use various distortion lenses…ripple effects… huge close-ups, etc.…to achieve a surreal, nightmarish aura as* ASHLAND *pushes through this mass of bodies in the smoke-choked room.*

*As he is pushing forward, voices assail him from all sides:*

VOICE #1: You can't get fingerprints off human skin.

VOICE #2: …so he took out the Luger and blew her head off.

VOICE #3: Like I told him—the X-rays destroyed his

white cells.

VOICE #4: They found her in the tub, strangled with a coat hanger.

VOICE #5: What I had, exactly, was a Grade Two epidermoid carcinoma at the base of a seborrheic keratosis.

VOICE #6: Potatoes have eyes. I really *believe* that.

VOICE #7: Big tiger moth! No blood inside…just like dust when I smashed him against the glass.

VOICE #8: Yeah, yeah…tied in a laundry bag in the car truck. Face was all blue.

VOICE #9: Five hundred seventy six murders in L.A. in 1977. Up to fifteen murders a week by '79…

VOICE #10: Med schools won't accept a dead body if it's more than twelve hours old.

VOICE #11: When a man is shot in the head his eyes go black.

VOICE #12: Never sign your name in blood.

*CLOSE ON* ASHLAND'S *FACE*

*sweating, filled with panic. His eyes seek out:*

*HIS POV*

*the huge Chinese gong, flaring gold from the far wall.*

*WIDE ON SCENE*

*as* ASHLAND *smashes his way through the partygoers to reach the gong.*

ASHLAND [*to himself, half-crazed*]: Got to…*stop* all this…

*With his full strength, he drives his right fist directly into the center of the bronze gong.*

*It* trembles *and* vibrates *under the blow. But there is NO SOUND FROM IT.*

*And no one at the party pays any attention whatever to* ASHLAND.

*ON* ASHLAND

*as he staggers back, stunned. The thin-faced cadaverous man leans in close to his ear.*

THIN MAN: No use, fella. You can't stop the party.

ASHLAND [*desperate*]: I'm…leaving…

THIN MAN [*with a chuckle*]: So go ahead. Nobody cares if you leave.

*CAMERA FOLLOWS* ASHLAND

*as he stumbles to the door, pulls it open, rushes into the hallway.*

*CAMERA TRACKS him to the elevator—where he frantically thumbs the "Down" button.*

*The doors slide open, and* ASHLAND *reacts to:*

LYDIA

*inside the elevator, smiling calmly.*

LYDIA: Been looking for me?

ASHLAND *enters in a daze, as the doors close behind him.*

INT. ELEVATOR

*as he stabs the "Lobby" button. The cage descends.*

ASHLAND: What's going on? That party...It's insane. Absolutely...horrible.

LYDIA [*amused*]: But, David, I thought you adored parties.

ASHLAND [*tight-faced*]: Let's just get out of this building. I've had enough.

*Suddenly, the elevator stops. Doors open again.*

ASHLAND'S *first wife,* TRISH, *steps inside, wearing a red-velvet party dress and carrying a martini.*

TRISH: Hi, lover! Long time no see.

ASHLAND is totally shocked. He stares at her.

TRISH [*takes a sip of the martini, makes a face*]: Ugh! No kick. That's the hell of it—all the booze is watered.

*And, in disgust, she tosses the glass into the elevator's wall mirror. It shatters.*

SMASH CUT TO:

SPLINTERED WINDSHIELD OF LIMO *(Accident scene)*—NIGHT

*In a series of FLASH FRAME CUTS we see twisted metal, broken bodies (*LYDIA *and* SIDNEY*)...and we see* ASHLAND *carried from the wreck to an ambulance—all in quick, fragmented images.*

BACK TO ELEVATOR SCENE

*as* ASHLAND *stares at his fractured reflection in the cracked mirror. The two women giggle behind him.*

ASHLAND [*numbly*]: That truck…on the freeway…

LYDIA: It hit us, David.

ASHLAND: And now we're all—

TRISH: *We* are, but not you. Not yet.

LYDIA: Don't fight it, David. Just let go.

TRISH: You're not going to make it…not back outside.

*Elevator stops. Doors open.*

*CAMERA FOLLOWS* ASHLAND *as he bolts for the outside doors, running across the wide, deserted lobby.*

*As he runs: quick FLASH FRAMES show him in a hospital bed, dying. SHOTS of doctor hovering over him, injecting stimulants, pounding his chest, etc.*

*At each of these FLASH FRAMES* DAVID *weakens, stumbles, falls, crawls toward the doors…*

ANGLE AT LOBBY DOORS

*as* ASHLAND *claws at the release bar, and the glass door* begins to open…

SMASH CUT TO:

INT. HOSPITAL ROOM—ON DAVID'S BED

*He lies unmoving under oxygen, eyes closed.*

*PAN TO "beeper" life-support machine by the bed— as the Lifeline suddenly ceases to register heart action. It* flattens *to an unbroken line across the screen.* ASHLAND'S *heart has stopped. The "beeping" is now CONTINUOUS.*

*BACK TO* ASHLAND.

*Just as the "beep" becomes continuous, in the* same *moment, the lobby doors* vanish *and the wall seals itself.*

*As* DAVID *claws for the doors that are no longer there we hear an O.S. giggle from the elevator behind him. (*TRISH *and* LYDIA *are amused.)*

ASHLAND, *now in panic, swings away from the wall, searching for a way out.*

*HIS P.O.V*

*Hallways—running off to either side of the main lobby.*

*CAMERA FOLLOWS him as he sets off in a frenzied run down one of the hallways, past a series of apartment doors...1D...1F...1J...*

*Exhausted, he falls against one of the doors, begins* pounding *on it.*

ASHLAND: Help me! Somebody, *help* me!

*ANGLE ON DOOR*

*as it is opened by the same* FAT MAN *we saw from the apartment ten floors above.*

FAT MAN [*with an evil smile*]: Hi, fella! C'mon in! [*beat*] Join the party.

*And we FREEZE FRAME on the man's smiling face.*

*FADE OUT*

# VI.

## SELLING YOUR WRITING

# FORTY ONE 41

## THE TRUTH ABOUT PUBLISHING:
### IT TAKES DETERMINATION

**W**riters yearn to see their words printed in books. Holding a book that contains *your* words, *your* thoughts, and expresses *your* imagination is a profound joy.

To achieve this, however, you must sell these words to a publisher. Meaning: you must submit a manuscript in the hope it will be accepted for publication. Thousands of novels are published each year, you tell yourself. Why not mine?

The odds are stacked heavily against you.

The suggested method of approaching a publisher—or a literary agent for that matter—with your novel is to send a proposal. This consists of a short cover letter explaining who you are and the genre of your novel, a one- to three-page synopsis of your book, and the first three chapters.

Publishers take a harder look at novel proposals submitted by *agents*. From experience, publishers have learned that if a reputable agent thinks enough of your work to submit it, there is a much greater possibility that it has the quality, depth, and marketing potential required for publication.

Every publisher deals with countless unsolicited, unagented proposals that arrive daily from eager novices who have found the publisher's address in a market guide. If your proposal has not been submitted by a reputable agent, it's going to wind up in what is called the *slush pile*.

The chances of a proposal from the slush pile being accepted for publication are minuscule. If such submissions are read at all (and they frequently are not), they are read not by busy editors, but by novice assistants or interns, often still in—or just out of—college, who have been delegated to perform this frustrating, usually thankless task.

If an assistant or intern comes across a proposal they like, something they see publishing potential in, they will start it along a complicated chain of editorial command. If your submission makes it to an actual editor's desk, you might have a shot.

It happens, but not often. Dashiell Hammett's first novel, *Red Harvest*, began as a slush pile submission, for example.

While publishers are gamblers, when they publish a book by an unknown author, they're taking a big gamble. They have to hope the book will sell enough copies to justify the faith and money they've invested in it, but the truth is: The majority of new books never earn back the author's advance payment, often very small, on future royalties. (An *advance against royalties* is the initial money an author receives upon signing the publishing contract.)

Even if you do get your novel published, you may not be happy with the result. Most new books are ignored by the critics, sell only a dismal number of copies, and soon vanish. Almost all first novels suffer this sad fate. (I was very fortunate, with my first novel, *Logan's Run*, that this did not happen.)

And within the last couple of decades, publishers have begun to rely increasingly on their authors to do the marketing for their books. Although all top publishers have marketing departments, their staffs are chronically underfunded and overworked—at least from the perspective of tyro authors. The top-selling authors at every house get full marketing attention—because those books generate the bucks that keep the house in business—while beginning authors may get none.

Some publishers now provide pamphlets of advice to new authors on how to market their books, marketing efforts that begin with that author's own local geographical area, areas of affiliation, and expertise.

Many of the genre organizations for writers, Sisters in Crime, whose members include mystery writers of both genders, as one example, go to considerable lengths to help their members become unpaid marketing executives for their own books. Authors' marketing efforts, on behalf of their own books, are often essential to success in today's publishing industry.

Common advice from both publishers and writers' organizations would be to get yourself interviewed or otherwise written up in your local newspapers and other local periodicals. Send review copies of your book to the proper reviewers at any publications you are somehow connected with, such as your union publication, which might publish a review or an announcement. Submit news squibs about your book to every organization you belong to. (Information on how to write news announcements and press releases is often available from the genre organizations.) Arrange to have yourself booked to speak in person to local service groups, as well as on your local radio, TV, and cable shows.

As soon as you obtain a contract from a publisher, begin making business acquaintances with the buyers and those who book authors for personal appearances at your local bookstores so when your book is published, you can arrange to do readings and signings at every local store within, say, a couple of hundred miles of your home—as well as any place you regularly visit, such as your vacation community, and places you travel to for business purposes.

So now you're feeling a bit deflated, right? You'd rather not hear about the odds of getting published or about the complex marketing tasks required of you.

If you're ever going to make it as a pro, these are the facts. Publishing is a competitive, tough business. You must develop the knowledge, skills and strength to succeed in it.

Talking to beginning writers over the decades of my career, I have come to admire the ones who tell me: "I don't care how tough this business is. It's not going to stop me. I'm going to show the world I can write!"

It's this kind of spirit—and the requisite talent—that will enable you to beat the odds.

# FORTY TWO 42

## LET'S TALK ABOUT AGENTS:
### CAVEAT EMPTOR

One of the two most frequent questions I'm asked is: "How do I get an agent?" (The other question is "Where do you get your ideas?")

Reputable agents are extremely busy professionals with souls of iron. They have no time for amateurs, particularly amateurs they judge to have little or no potential. Often they won't even bother to tell you to get lost if you write them asking about possible representation.

It's a Catch-22 situation: You can't get an agent to represent you unless you are already a professional writer, and you can't become a professional writer without an agent.

So, as a beginning writer, what do you do?

One approach is to submit your stories to small, non-paying magazines. Keep at it until you get three to five stories published, then check the list of agents in one of the market guides such as *Writer's Market*. The problem with doing this is that some of the agents listed in the market guides are not necessarily completely professional in the way they conduct their business. Some others operate—in effect—as two different agencies: one for professional writers, and another for wannabe writers of varied potential and talent—with different agents dealing with these two diverse categories of writers.

In my opinion, the best way to obtain an agent for your prose work is to create business friendships with writers who are already of professional stature. Try organizations of genre writers. The Mystery Writers of America is one good place to make such contacts. (See the Resources for Writers section at the back of this book.) If fellow pros like and respect your work, they'll often recommend you to their agent as someone the agency ought to sign. This approach has the additional advantage of having someone you know personally confirm that the agency operates in a professional manner. Throughout my career, I have been recommended to several agencies by friends who were already represented by those agents.

Another possibility is to check the acknowledgements sections of books that are similar to your own work. Frequently, these pages will thank the agent and the agencies who made the sale of those books possible, and you will then have some assurance that this particular agent, at this particular agency, is competent. Naturally, those writers who are constantly on the top of the best-seller lists are represented by top agents who may have no interest in representing *you*, so read the book review sections in *Publishers Weekly* (check your local library for copies). Read the reviews of works similar to your own by lesser-known writers, and then check out the books themselves at your bookstore or library to see if the agent is acknowledged.

When you sign with an agency, and they negotiate a contract on your behalf with a publisher, the agency will subsequently receive all checks intended *for you*, although the checks will be made out *to them*. They deposit the checks into their bank account, then cut new checks—less the agency commission—and forward these new checks, drawn on their own agency bank account, to you.

Generally, your signature on the representation contract agrees that this agency will represent this particular property for many years or what may amount to perpetuity, which means that decades in the future, you will still be depending on this particular agency to negotiate new sales on these older projects and to receive checks for you even if you have moved on to other agents or agencies in the meantime. It is, therefore, extremely important to choose the right agent and agency—from the very beginning of your career. Often a writer's first sales, for little or no money, become *big money* projects in future years, as the writer's reputation grows. Since you'll likely still be with this same agency for these early career properties, choose as well as you possibly can.

The general procedure is to mail an agent (or agency) copies of your *published* work, along with a brief, one-page letter—never longer—asking if they would be interested in representing you. If you don't hear from them in a reasonable time (say, six weeks), try again with another agent or agency.

If you want to be a scriptwriter, or you want to sell film/TV rights to your prose work, you need to know that all agents and agencies whose clients' work is subject to the Writers Guild of America, west (WGAw) Minimum Basic Agreement (MBA) with *producers*, are required to be signatories to the WGAw *agency* MBA. To find out if a particular agent or agency is a signatory, contact the WGAw. (See the Resources for Writers section at the back of this book).

Members of the WGAw (as I am) can *only* sell film/TV rights to their work through agents and agencies who are MBA signatories; this is a hard-won guarantee of an agency's financial stability and professionalism that is gratefully appreciated by every industry writer I know.

You can also talk to agents in person at writing conferences and publishing conventions in the hopes that one of them might be open to taking a chance on you and your work. Many important business relationships are forged at these events and such meetings are one of the best ways for beginning writers to launch business relationships with reputable agents.

Never forget that agents are in business to make money. If they don't think you have money-making potential for them, they will not take you on. If they do take you on and you subsequently don't prove yourself to their satisfaction, they will drop you.

It's up to you to convince them that your determination, courage, and talent are of professional caliber, and that the potential for you to make money *for them* actually exists.

# FORTY THREE 43

## EGO:
## DON'T DENY IT—NURTURE IT!

I'm going to speak of ego here in its popular usage as self-esteem (rather than in the formal terms of academic psychology, where the ego—together with the id and the superego—comprise the psyche).

Self-esteem is essential at every level of growth and health, yet we are part of a culture that has historically deprecated nearly everything that has the capacity to increase our psychological, emotional, spiritual, physical, sexual, and creative health. Many of us (myself included) grew up in families, religions, geographical areas, and socioeconomic groups where we were taught that the ideal human being is humble and self-effacing and never boasts of his or her accomplishments. The purpose of this teaching was to constrain—even crush—our budding self-esteem so we would become malleable, controllable adults who would unquestionably accept what authority (whatever that might have consisted of during our formative years) told us was right, moral, ethical, and correct.

For most of us, this negative conditioning became—to some measure, great or small—one of the primary lenses through which we regard ourselves as adults. Destructive to all, this internalized sense of ourselves can prove particularly devastating to the beginning writer.

At the outset, before you experience editorial recognition, acceptance, or sales, your self-esteem is usually all you have to sustain you. It is a necessity. Without it, you can be destroyed by rejection—defeated before the battle has begun. And one must fight and win many battles in order to become a professional writer.

A strong sense of self-esteem, of self-worth, must prevail in the novice writer. If you don't believe in yourself and your talent, no one else will believe in you.

At least from my early twenties, I had a steady voice deep inside me that said: "I have talent. I will never give up. I will succeed." That inner voice kept me going. It was always there, regardless of what the outer circumstances of my life appeared to be at that moment.

As a writer, do not tolerate anyone telling you to be humble. Without an abiding sense of self-esteem, you won't be able to survive the often difficult realities of professional writing. When an editor returns a story that you're certain is good, you must assure yourself that the person was mistaken in rejecting you and that the story will sell elsewhere. (*Star Wars* was rejected by eight studios before George Lucas found one that would produce it.)

Tell yourself: "I am good and I *know* it. And someday soon, others will discover just how good I really am."

Despair and self-pity are not options on the road to success. Build your ego—your sense of self-estcem—as a wall to protect yourself from editorial assault and indifference.

Your sense of self-worth can be your best, most loyal supporter the truest friend a writer may ever have.

## VERSATILITY:
### A BLESSING OR A PROBLEM?

Over the course of my career, I have discovered that the capacity for versatility—having the ability to switch genres and formats with relative ease—can be both a blessing and a problem.

Examine the careers of successful, big-money authors. You will discover that most built their reputations (and their financial security) book to book, and within a single genre. This is true of practically all of the best-selling writers. They did not (as I have done) jump constantly from one field to another.

*Logan's Run* is science fiction, but I followed it up with two mystery novels, *Death Is for Losers* and *The White Cad Cross-Up*.

My *Rio Renegades* is a western. *Helltracks* is a horror novel. *Life at the Edge* is a biography. *Carnival of Speed* is a collection of pieces about auto racing. *Dashiell Hammett: A Casebook* is a critical study. *Dark Encounters* is a collection of my verse. *The Ray Bradbury Companion* is a bibliography. *Ships in the Night* is a collection of mainstream stories. *California Sorcery* is an edited anthology of fantasy. *Death Drive* is an original action screenplay. *Ill Met By Moonlight* features my artwork.

When Tim Sinniger profiled me in *Firsts* (the magazine for book collectors), he described me as "one of the most versatile and productive talents of this century, and if you think that's hyperbole, just consider [Nolan's] credits as novelist, short story writer, poet, biographer, literary critic, speech writer, lecturer, essayist, technical writer, editor, bibliographer, columnist, film and television script writer, actor, teacher, and cartoonist/illustrator." I have been both blessed and challenged by an insatiable desire—a compulsion, really—to leap from one subject to the next, and from genre to genre. Yes, I've kept myself excited by what I've written. I have satisfied a constant need to explore new arenas. I have continually met fresh challenges with prose, scripting, and verse, but I have never remained long enough in any one field to build a major reputation within that field.

Today I regret this. I now wish it had been otherwise. But, since my personal passion as a writer has propelled me into multiple fields of creativity, regret is futile. I take pride in the literary worlds I have conquered and in the awards I have won.

I also know that, if I had to start over as a writer, I would probably follow the same twisting road. It's rooted in who I am and what I continue to be.

All of which is to warn you, as a beginning writer, *not* to follow my example. You will be much better served if you choose a single field compatible with your interests and talents and then build your reputation book to book within that field.

Back in the late 1960s, for *The Writer*, I gloried in my versatility:

> I continually seed my subconscious, then harvest what grows from the planting. I refuse to limit myself, pin labels on my work, allow myself to go sour, go stale, dry up creatively. I'm never bored with writing because I use versatility to the full.

All true. But now I no longer celebrate that versatility. My unlimited range has, ironically, become my greatest career limitation.

So, if your personality and talent allow you to be a single-genre writer, my advice is to choose a field you are truly interested in and then stick with it.

As for me, I will keep on doing what I've done for over fifty years: continue to explore new literary worlds. My versatility has proven to be both a blessing *and* a problem in my career, but the most important thing is: My versatility is *me*.

# FORTY FIVE 45

## SELF-DISCIPLINE FULL TIME:
### GIVING UP YOUR DAY JOB

You've made some sales—enough to convince yourself that you've reached a professional level and it's okay to quit your day job. You've saved enough money—and, if necessary, reduced both your expenditures and any indebtedness—to get you through at least one year. You're excited, ready to plunge into that uncharted sea of words. You're ready to write on a full-time basis.

Beware! The discipline that enabled you to report to work at a certain time each morning for your job: gone. When I worked in an office, my boss had a fit if I was five minutes late. The discipline from outside that kept you working for a set number of hours every working day is no longer going to exist. You're on your own time now, and you are your own boss.

As your own boss, you must now be tough on yourself with regard to your writing. You must actually *write* for a minimum of three or four hours *every day*, leaving your other waking hours free for reading, analyzing, and research.

Being a professional is about getting publishable words *on paper*.

Stephen King writes every day.

Dean Koontz writes every day.

Ray Bradbury writes every day.

I write every day.

No excuses. No slacking off because you're "not in the mood" or because you're "not inspired."

Nonsense!

If you can't achieve the self-discipline necessary to get the words out each and every day, then you'd better forget about becoming a pro and stick to your office job.

At least your boss won't put up with excuses.

By the way, I highly recommend *The Intrinsic Exerciser: Discovering the Joy of Exercise* by Jay Kimiecik. Although Kimiecik's book is obviously about physical activity, the philosophy, discussion of psychological and emotional challenges, and extremely practical techniques presented in this book are directly applicable to the discipline and development of habits required for a successful, full-time writing career.

## HOW TO COPE WITH REJECTION:
### KEEP WRITING, KEEP TRYING

Every writer faces rejection at one time or another. After more than 400 printed stories, Ray Bradbury still gets rejected. I have had 165 stories in print, and I still get rejected. Rejections don't stop when you begin to sell. They keep coming, at intervals, throughout your career.

Case in point: In 1983 I wrote a story called "Ceremony," about a killer-for-hire trapped in a small Rhode Island town who becomes victim to a bizarre annual ceremony. It was written to order for an upcoming anthology, edited by a friend who admired my work. He sent the story back. A flat rejection. Claimed it wasn't "up to [my] standard," that the atmosphere was "not spooky enough," and that the story was essentially a failure.

I knew he was dead wrong about "Ceremony." I was certain it was one of my strongest shock tales and that the atmosphere was indeed "spooky enough." Undaunted, that same day I sent it to Charles Grant, a veteran editor who was putting together a new anthology titled *Midnight*. He accepted it with enthusiasm, and—to my delight—"Ceremony" was subsequently chosen for *The Year's Best Horror Stories*. I'd been vindicated twice over!

But there's more…

Just this week, as I was working on this book, I received a phone call informing me that "Ceremony" is now being taught in a college course on the short story, and it is being presented as a top-notch example of shock fiction.

I recently received a rejection because the editor said he didn't print ghost stories. I sent the manuscript back to him, pointing out that my tale was *not* a ghost story, that the figure he had identified as a ghost was actually the mental projection of a sick mind, but I wasn't able to convince him. He refused to reconsider the story—and I sold it on the next mailing.

If one of my stories is rejected, I submit it elsewhere *that same day*. I never allow a rejection to impede the forward flow of my submissions.

But how do *you* handle rejection?

If you believe in your talent, you must never allow rejection to destroy you. Beyond the quality of your work, there are many reasons an editor may reject a manuscript: Your story doesn't fit the particular needs of a magazine or book; the editor may have recently purchased a story with a plot similar to yours; the editor may have a bias against the subject matter of your tale; or the editor may simply have failed to understand what you've written.

I was key speaker at a recent writing conference in Tucson, Arizona, and a sad-eyed woman approached me. She'd tried writing, she said, but the rejections were so depressing she'd given up. "That was ten years ago," she told me, "and I haven't written anything since."

A tragic admission. She had allowed rejection to destroy what might have been a successful writing career.

Don't let rejection destroy you. Keep writing. Keep trying. Keep developing your skills.

If you have talent, your work *will* find a home.

# RESOURCES FOR WRITERS

**To find an agent:**

*Writer's Market*
www.writersmarket.com

*Publishers Weekly* (magazine)
www.publishersweekly.com

*Independent Publisher* (online magazine)
www.independentpublisher.com
This is a good source of marketing information of interest to authors.

**Scriptwriting:**

Samuel French Theatre & Film Bookshops
7623 Sunset Blvd.
Hollywood CA 90046
(323) 876-0570
samuelfrench@earthlink.net
Books on all aspects of the entertainment industry, including scriptwriting and script formatting.

Writers Guild of America, west [WGAw]
7000 West Third Street
Los Angeles CA 90048
(323) 951-4000

www.wga.org

A pamphlet, "Guide to the Guild," is available at no cost to those who are not members of the WGAw. Phone the Membership Section at (323) 782-4532.

Check the WGAw website for agencies and agents who are signatories to the WGAw Minimum Basic Agreement ( WGAw MBA).

Prior to negotiating or selling film rights to any of your properties, phone the WGAw Signatories Department at (323) 782-4514 to determine if a producer or a production company is a signatory to the WGAw MBA. If not, use extreme caution because virtually all legitimate producers and production companies are WGAw signatories. Regardless of whether you are or are not a WGAw member, dealing exclusively with WGAw signatories will provide you with a measure of automatic and fundamental protection due to Guild requirements which all signatories to the MBA must comply with.

The WGAw publishes *Written By*, a print magazine published several times a year for its members. Subscriptions are automatically entered for WGAw members. Paid subscriptions (including a discounted rate for qualified students) are available to non-members and single copies are available for purchase. The offices of Written By are located at the above WGAw address. Phone: (323) 782-4522. Email: writtenby@wga.org

**Writers associations:**

Mystery Writers of America
www.mysterywriters.org

Romance Writers of America
www.rwanational.org

Science Fiction & Fantasy Writers of America, Inc.
www.sfwa.org
Sisters in Crime
www.sistersincrime.org

Western Writers of America
www.westernwriters.org

**Of special note:**

*The Paris Review* was founded in 1953 by a group of gifted Americans, led by the late George Plimpton, and is still being published today. Each issue contains an interview with a well-known novelist, poet, or playwright. These interviews have been collected in a series of books under the overall title *Writers at Work: The Paris Review Interviews*. The first five volumes were all published in the United States by Viking Press between 1958 and 1981. Malcolm Cowley edited the first in the series, and George Plimpton edited numbers two through five.

Seventy-five writers were interviewed for these initial five volumes, and they are books I urge all writers to seek out and read. Many of the quotations in the opening section, "Wise Words from the Masters," were gleaned from these collections. Although now out of print, they are well worth running down on the Internet.

Each interview offers rare and fascinating insights into the writer's life. They are brilliant, soul-searching, and deeply revealing, and I consider them required reading for anyone who hopes to write professionally.

Look 'em up. You won't be sorry.

# INDEX

# ABOUT THE AUTHOR

William F. Nolan has been widely published in a dozen fields, including science fiction, mystery, auto racing, Westerns, dark fantasy, biography, and mainstream fiction. Internationally famous for his genre classic *Logan's Run* (best-selling novel, MGM film, CBS television series, and mega-budget remake from Warner Bros.), Nolan has achieved some 1,500 sales since his first short story was printed in 1954. He has eighty books to his credit, including fifteen story collections and a dozen novels. Translated around the world, Nolan's work has been printed in over three hundred anthologies and textbooks (including *Best Detective Stories of the Year*, *Best of the West*, *Year's Best Science Fiction*, *The Year's Best Fantasy*, *Best Motor Racing Stories*, *Dark Crimes: Great Noir Fiction*, and *New Masterpieces of Horror*). Nolan has also written extensively for films and television (*Burnt Offerings*, *Trilogy of Terror*, *The Turn of the Screw*, *Melvin Purvis: G-Man*, etc.).

His critically acclaimed *How to Write Horror Fiction* (from *Writer's Digest Books*) helped establish his credentials as an expert guide to beginning writers. He has taught creative writing at Bowling Green State College in Ohio and (in 2005) at Central Oregon Community College. Nolan has participated as a staff member of the Sandhills Writers Conference in Augusta, Georgia, and at Wrangling With Writing in Tucson, Arizona.

An accomplished speaker, Nolan has lectured extensively. He has spoken at the University of California at Berkeley, the Detroit Institute of Arts, UCLA in Southern California, at the main library in Los Angeles to the Young Adult Librarians, and at the Writers' Week at Pasadena City College in California.

Recipient of many awards (including an honorary doctorate), his work has been cited for excellence by the Library Association of America and praised by such noted colleagues as Stephen King, Ray Bradbury, Dean Koontz, Peter Straub, and Robert Bloch. Nolan is twice winner of the Edgar Allan Poe Special Award from the Mystery Writers of America. Among his other awards are two Golden Medallions from Europe, the San Francisco Maltese Falcon Award, a Distinguished Career Commendation from the City of Los Angeles, and the "Living Legend" Award from the International Horror Guild. In 2006 he was voted "Author Emeritus" by the Science Fiction Writers of America.

Incredibly versatile, Nolan has also been a technical writer (on ophthalmology), an editor (at four magazines, and on numerous anthologies), and he has written for the stage, for radio, and for Walt Disney comic magazines. He is a respected authority on the hard-boiled genre, with such books to his credit as *The Black Mask Boys* and *Hammett: A Life at the Edge.*

A longtime resident of Los Angeles, Nolan is currently on temporary assignment in Bend, Oregon, where he is working on new novels and stories.

Nolan's two Websites are: www.williamfnolan.com and www.nolansworld.com.

*For a host of books on writing,*

*please visit*

*QuillDriverBooks.com*